Early United States

HARCOURT BRACE SOCIAL STUDIES

READING SUPPORT
AND TEST PREPARATION

HARCOURT BRACE & COMPANY
Orlando Atlanta Austin Boston San Francisco Chicago Dallas
New York Toronto London

Visit The Learning Site at http://www.hbschool.com

Copyright © by Harcourt Brace & Company

All rights reserved. No part of this publication may be reproduced or transmitted in any form or by any means, electronic or mechanical, including photocopy, recording, or any information storage and retrieval system.

Teachers using HARCOURT BRACE SOCIAL STUDIES may photocopy complete pages in sufficient quantities for classroom use only and not for resale.

HARCOURT BRACE and Quill Design is a registered trademark of Harcourt Brace & Company.

Printed in the United States of America

ISBN 0-15-312384-2

8 9 10 073 01

Contents

UNIT 1

The Ancient Americas
A-B-C Lesson Plan—Buried Treasure	1
Anticipation Guide	2
Buried Treasure	3
Standardized-Test-Format Questions	4
A-B-C Lesson Plan—Corn—The Bread of Life	5
Word Splash	6
Corn—The Bread of Life	7
Standardized-Test-Format Questions	8

UNIT 2

Explorations and Encounters
A-B-C Lesson Plan—A Dangerous Crossing	9
Word Splash	10
A Dangerous Crossing	11
Standardized-Test-Format Questions	12
A-B-C Lesson Plan—The Story of Chocolate	13
Anticipation Guide	14
The Story of Chocolate	15
Standardized-Test-Format Questions	16

UNIT 3

Our Colonial Heritage
A-B-C Lesson Plan—Barn Raising	17
Word Splash	18
Barn Raising	19
Standardized-Test-Format Questions	20
A-B-C Lesson Plan—School Days	21
Anticipation Guide	22
School Days	23
Standardized-Test-Format Questions	24

UNIT 4

The American Revolution

A-B-C Lesson Plan—Benjamin Franklin: Writer, Scientist, Statesman	25
Anticipation Guide	26
Benjamin Franklin: Writer, Scientist, Statesman	27
Standardized-Test-Format Questions	28
A-B-C Lesson Plan—The Spirit of 1776	29
Word Splash	30
The Spirit of 1776	31
Standardized-Test-Format Questions	32

UNIT 5

The New Nation

A-B-C Lesson Plan—Father of the Constitution	33
Anticipation Guide	34
Father of the Constitution	35
Standardized-Test-Format Questions	36
A-B-C Lesson Plan—Abigail Adams, A Woman Ahead of Her Time	37
Word Splash	38
Abigail Adams, A Woman Ahead of Her Time	39
Standardized-Test-Format Questions	40

UNIT 6

Our Nation Grows

A-B-C Lesson Plan—Gold Fever	41
Anticipation Guide	42
Gold Fever	43
Standardized-Test-Format Questions	44
A-B-C Lesson Plan—An American Story	45
Word Splash	46
An American Story	47
Standardized-Test-Format Questions	48

UNIT 7

War Divides the Nation

A-B-C Lesson Plan—Balloons in Battle	49
Word Splash	50
Balloons in Battle	51
Standardized-Test-Format Questions	52
A-B-C Lesson Plan—Abraham Lincoln, White House Father	53
Anticipation Guide	54
Abraham Lincoln, White House Father	55
Standardized-Test-Format Questions	56

UNIT 8

Americans, Then and Now

A-B-C Lesson Plan—Bell's Telephone	57
Word Splash	58
Bell's Telephone	59
Standardized-Test-Format Questions	60
A-B-C Lesson Plan—Edison's Talking Machine	61
Anticipation Guide	62
Edison's Talking Machine	63
Standardized-Test-Format Questions	64

Item Analyses and Answer Keys	65
Reading Comprehension Strategies	70
Hands-On Activity	74
Blackline Copying Masters	75

Introduction

The articles in *Reading Support and Test Preparation* relate to the units in Harcourt Brace's *United States*. There are two articles for each unit. The articles have been designed to provide high-interest, motivating reading experiences that expand on or spring from a person's life, an event, or a topic that is presented in the unit. In most instances, the articles contain some of the vocabulary words from the unit so that students have an opportunity to reinforce key vocabulary.

There are a number of ways that you can use the articles. You may wish to use the articles after you have completed the unit in *United States,* in which students are exposed to background information about the topic. You may also use the articles before students read the unit, as a way to provide background. You may want to read aloud the articles to students, or you may wish to have students use the articles as a test-simulation experience.

Each article is preceded by a three-part, A-B-C Lesson Plan (Access, Build, and Close), which provides a simple procedure for using the article. An Anticipation Guide or a Word Splash blackline master is included with the plan for students to use before reading the article. These copying masters can be used to help build interest, activate prior knowledge, and set purposes for reading. The lesson plan also includes a related cross-curricular activity in language arts, mathematics, science, health, or art.

At the end of each article are eight standardized-test-format questions. These questions can help you assess students' reading comprehension skills. In addition, the questions include strategies often tested at this grade level, such as identifying the best summary, identifying cause and effects, and using context clues.

Item analyses and answer keys are provided at the back of the book to assist you with evaluation. Also at the back of this book are descriptions of several useful reading comprehension strategies that you can use with the articles. Several blackline masters of word webs, diagrams, and charts suitable for duplication are also included.

Reading Support and Test Preparation has been designed to provide:
- additional motivating reading experiences for your students.
- content related to units in *Early United States*.
- opportunities to build background and reinforce reading skills.
- practice opportunities for standardized tests.
- reading strategy activities to help students organize information.

CONVERSION CHART FOR SCORING

After students have read the article and answered the questions, you can use the following chart to determine a grade.

Correct Number of Responses	Percentage Score
8	100%
7	88%
6	75%
5	63%
4	50%
3	38%
2	25%
1	13%

UNIT 1
Buried Treasure

A·B·C LESSON PLANNER

1. Access

- **READING STRATEGY:** Use the Anticipation Guide on page 2 before having small groups of students read the article. Write the statements on the board, or use the sheet as a copying master. Invite students to tell whether they agree or disagree with each statement. They can write their responses in their journals or learning logs. Do not expect students to know the answers. This activity is designed to help build interest, activate prior knowledge, and set purposes for reading.

2. Build

- Have students read the article, or read it aloud to them.
- As students read or after they finish reading the article, they may change their opinions about the statements. If they do, have them discuss why they revised their opinions, and have them state what they learned from their reading that allowed them to confirm or revise their opinions.

3. Close

- Have students complete the standardized-test-format questions after they read the article. (An item analysis that identifies the test objectives covered by each question, as well as an answer key, can be found on page 65.)
- **LANGUAGE ARTS ACTIVITY:** Have students conduct research to find five facts about the Olmecs. Students may wish to use their facts to create an Olmec Fact-Finding Game.

Name _____ Date _____

Buried Treasure
Anticipation Guide

Check One

	Agree	Disagree
1. The Olmecs lived more than 2,000 years ago.		
2. Archaeologists are scientists who study the stars in the night sky.		
3. Olmec temples indicate that religion was an important part of Olmec life.		
4. Olmec artifacts indicate that the Olmecs made musical instruments out of wood and clay.		
5. Olmec artifacts tell us very little about the Olmec civilization.		

BURIED TREASURE

In the 1860s, a Mexican farmer began clearing a patch of land for farming. Before he was through, he had discovered evidence of an ancient civilization! Buried deep under the ground was a giant stone head almost 5 feet high and more than 2,000 years old. It was the first Olmec artifact ever found. For archaeologists it was an invitation to solve a mystery: Who were the Olmec people, and how did they live?

Like detectives, archaeologists use clues to solve mysteries about people who lived long ago. Some of their most important clues are artifacts from the past. To learn more about the Olmecs, archaeologists began looking for more artifacts. Each discovery gave information about the culture of these ancient people.

For example, archaeologists found that some temples had been built on top of pyramids. This showed them that religion was an important part of Olmec life. Archaeologists also found that jaguars were often in Olmec art and on other artifacts. This told them that the large, spotted cat played an important role in Olmec religion.

The huge stone head found by the Mexican farmer may have been the statue of an Olmec ruler. This is probably the case because similar heads were later found, each "wearing" a helmet with a special symbol. The symbol might have been the name of the ruler.

Archaeologists have found that the Olmec culture was based on farming. Their main crops were corn, beans, and squash. How did archaeologists discover this? By examining the remains of Olmec trash!

Artifacts also provide clues about what the Olmecs did for entertainment. The people played games with balls made from the sap of rubber trees. They made flutes and other musical instruments out of wood and clay.

Archaeologists believe that the Olmecs traveled to other parts of present-day Mexico, Central America, and the coast of the Gulf of Mexico to *barter*. There is evidence of this trading of goods with other people because Olmec artifacts have been found buried in places far from Olmec lands.

Like artifacts from every civilization, those left by the Olmecs are buried treasures that unlock mysteries of the past. What artifacts will we leave behind? And what will they reveal about us to the people of the future?

Name _____ Date _____

Buried Treasure

Choose the best answer and mark the letter of your choice.

1. What is this article mostly about?
    A. how detectives solve mysteries
    B. how archaeologists study Olmec artifacts
    C. what the Olmec religion taught
    D. how historians find artifacts today

2. In the 1860s, a Mexican farmer discovered
    F. evidence of the Anasazis.
    G. a 500-year-old Mayan artifact.
    H. a cave painting of animals.
    J. the first Olmec artifact ever found.

3. The discovery of a giant stone head caused archaeologists to
    A. begin studying the Olmec civilization.
    B. think that the Olmecs were part of the Aztec Empire.
    C. determine that the Olmecs lived more than 10,000 years ago.
    D. conclude that the Mayas conquered the Olmecs.

4. What caused archaeologists to think that religion was an important part of Olmec life?
    F. Rulers wore helmets with special symbols.
    G. Some temples were built on top of pyramids.
    H. Artifacts were found in trash.
    J. Olmec art included pictures of jaguars.

5. According to the article, archaeologists have learned from artifacts that the Olmecs
    A. built special rooms for ceremonies.
    B. used sap from rubber trees for food.
    C. made musical instruments out of wood and clay.
    D. wrote about jaguars.

6. In this article, the word *barter* means
    F. to travel to other places.
    G. to study ancient religions.
    H. to trade goods with others.
    J. to search for artifacts.

7. According to the article, artifacts are "buried treasures" because they
    A. are interesting to archaeologists.
    B. provide valuable information about the past.
    C. are buried very deep beneath the Earth's surface.
    D. are extremely difficult to find.

8. What will people of the future probably do with the artifacts we leave behind?
    F. bury them
    G. trade them
    H. hide them
    J. study them

UNIT 1
Corn—The Bread of Life

A·B·C *L*ESSON *P*LANNER

1. *A*ccess

- **READING STRATEGY:** Use the Word Splash on page 6 to help students make predictions about the article. Write the words on the board, or use the sheet as a copying master. Invite students to predict how each word or phrase relates to corn and Native American cultures. Students can write their predictions in their journals or learning logs. Do not expect students to know the answers. This activity is designed to help build interest, activate prior knowledge, and set purposes for reading.

2. *B*uild

- Have students read the article, or read it aloud to them.
- As students read or after they finish reading the article, they may change their Word Splash predictions. Have them identify which predictions are correct, and have them state what they have learned from reading the article.

3. *C*lose

- Have students complete the standardized-test-format questions after they read the article. (An item analysis that identifies the test objectives covered by each question, as well as an answer key, can be found on page 65.)
- **MATHEMATICS ACTIVITY:** Have students find recipes for succotash or corn bread and figure out the amount of each ingredient that would be needed to serve 4 people, 12 people, and the whole class.

Name _____ Date _____

Corn—The Bread of Life

Word Splash

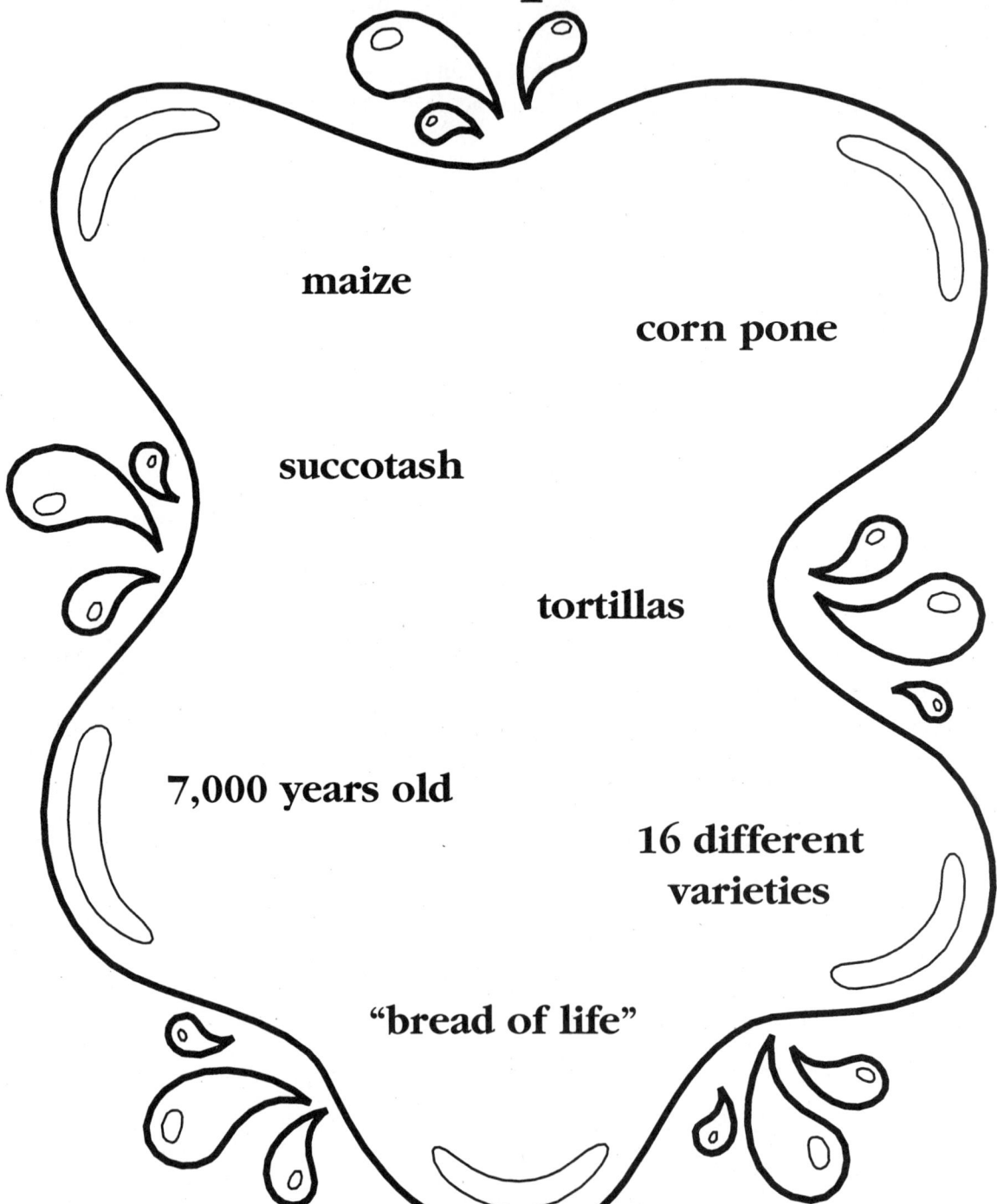

maize

corn pone

succotash

tortillas

7,000 years old

16 different varieties

"bread of life"

CORN
The Bread of Life

Indians throughout the Americas called corn *maize,* a word that has two meanings: "grain of the gods" and "bread of life." Both meanings show how important corn was in Native American cultures. In fact, it was so important that Indians rarely went to war during the growing season. They were too busy planting, *cultivating,* and harvesting their corn. Taking care of their plants before harvesting was very important.

The Indians of the Eastern Woodlands often planted corn and beans together. The corn plant gave support to the bean vines, which climbed the tall stalks. When the corn and beans were ripe, they were cooked together in water, sometimes with fish or meat. The result was a stew known as *sukquttahash.* Today we call it succotash. In winter, the same dish was made from either dried corn and beans or frozen vegetables. To use frozen succotash, an Indian cook chopped off a chunk of it and cooked it over a fire. It was an early version of frozen food!

The most common ingredient in Native American cooking was *cornmeal.* It was made by grinding or pounding dried corn into powder. The cornmeal could then be used as flour for baking.

Mexican Indians used cornmeal to make thin, flat pancakes. The Spanish called the pancakes *tortillas,* meaning "little cakes." In the North, cornmeal cakes became known as corn pone.

Over time, Native Americans developed many different kinds of corn. The Hopis, for example, grew at least 16 different varieties, each for a particular purpose. Some kinds grew well in the desert because they needed little water. Other types could be dried and stored for use during *droughts,* for it was important to have food for these long periods of dry weather. And still other types of corn were good for eating fresh. These types were often eaten as corn on the cob—a quick, tasty meal that could be cooked and eaten in the fields during harvesttime.

One of the oldest known types of corn is popcorn. Archaeologists have found the fluffy white kernels preserved in dry caves. They have also found unpopped kernels that are about 7,000 years old. What happened when the archaeologists dropped the kernels into hot oil? They popped, of course!

Name _____ Date _____

Corn—The Bread of Life

Choose the best answer and mark the letter of your choice.

1. What is this article mostly about?
   A. Native American religions
   B. corn in Native American cultures
   C. cornmeal in Native American foods
   D. Native American popcorn

2. In this article, the word *cultivating* means
   F. planting crops.
   G. farming.
   H. harvesting crops.
   J. taking care of crops.

3. Native Americans rarely went to war during the growing season because they
   A. were busy in the cornfields.
   B. had plenty of food to eat.
   C. were busy hunting and fishing.
   D. spent a great deal of their time trading with other Indians.

4. According to the article, the main foods in succotash are
   F. meat and fish.
   G. corn pone and tortillas.
   H. corn and beans.
   J. cornmeal and carrots.

5. According to the article, Indians of the Eastern Woodlands preserved food by
   A. storing it in the ground.
   B. boiling it.
   C. drying or freezing it.
   D. adding water to it.

6. In this article, the word *cornmeal* means
   F. a dish made from corn.
   G. dried corn soaked in water.
   H. little cakes made from corn.
   J. dried corn ground into powder.

7. What is the main idea of the fifth paragraph?
   A. Native Americans developed 16 varieties of corn.
   B. Native Americans developed different kinds of corn for different purposes.
   C. The Hopis ate corn on the cob every year during harvesttime.
   D. Corn could be stored easily for long periods of time.

8. In this article, the word *drought* means a long period of
   F. dry weather.
   G. cold weather.
   H. hot weather.
   J. rainy weather.

8 • Unit 1

UNIT 2
A Dangerous Crossing

A·B·C Lesson Planner

1. Access

- **READING STRATEGY:** Use the Word Splash on page 10 to help students make predictions about the article. Write the words on the board, or use the sheet as a copying master. Read the words in the Word Splash with the students. Invite students to predict how each word or phrase relates to sailing to the Americas. Students can write their predictions in their journals or learning logs. Do not expect students to know the answers. This activity is designed to help build interest, activate prior knowledge, and set purposes for reading.

2. Build

- Have students read the article, or read it aloud to them.
- As students read or after they finish reading the article, they may change their Word Splash predictions. Have them identify the predictions that were correct, and have them state what they have learned from reading the article.

3. Close

- Have students complete the standardized-test-format questions after they read the article. (An item analysis that identifies the test objectives covered by each question, as well as an answer key, can be found on page 65.)

- **MATHEMATICS ACTIVITY:** Have students conduct research to find the distance covered by the *Mayflower* on its voyage. Invite them to create word problems that use the distance covered and the number of days the voyage took.

Name _____ Date _____

A Dangerous Crossing
Word Splash

Pilgrims

Mayflower

salt pork and hardtack

"Man overboard!"

storms

seasick

waves crashed over the ship

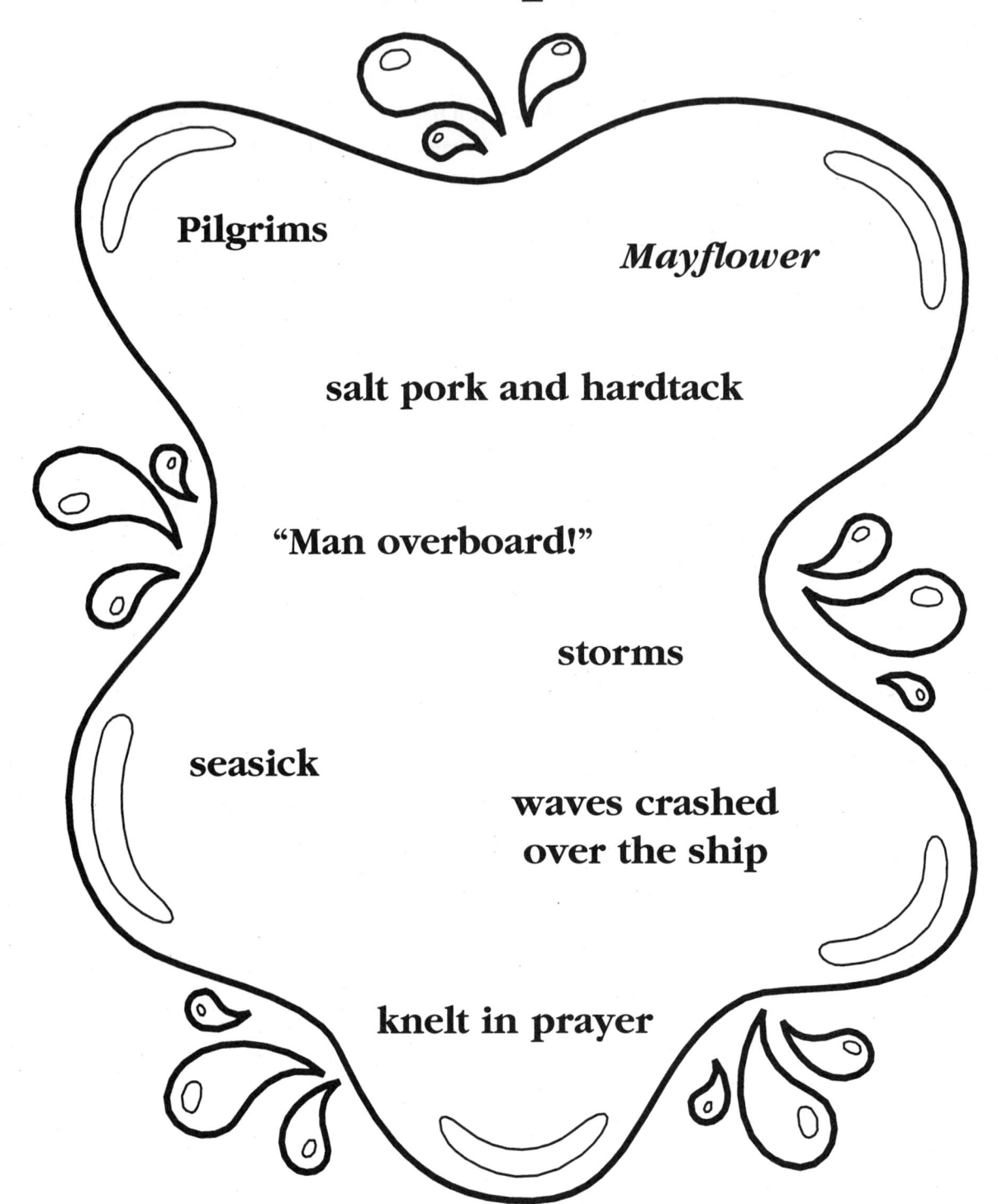

knelt in prayer

A Dangerous Crossing

On September 16, 1620, the *Mayflower* left England, bound for the Americas. On board were about 100 Pilgrims, plus 30 sailors. The *Mayflower* was not designed to carry so many people. In fact, the Pilgrims had planned to make the journey in two ships. But one of the ships turned out to be unfit for the *expedition*. Therefore, all the Pilgrims had to sail in one crowded ship.

The passengers on the *Mayflower* were crowded into a small area below the main deck. There they ate, prayed, and slept. There was no privacy and hardly any light. Even worse, there was no fresh air.

In good weather, the passengers could go up on deck for exercise and air. But in bad weather, they had to stay below. For most of the trip, the weather was terrible.

The storms began in October and continued for the rest of the voyage. Waves crashed over the ship, flooding the main deck. The *seasick* Pilgrims huddled together, praying, while water poured down from the deck above. Made sick by the pitching of the ship, the Pilgrims were miserable.

During one storm the main beam in the middle of the ship cracked. It had to be fixed, or the ship would sink. The question was how to repair it. Everyone had a different idea. Finally, the captain made a decision. Luckily, it was the right one. If it had been wrong, the colony of Plymouth might never have been founded.

During another storm, the passengers heard a terrifying cry: "Man overboard!" One of the Pilgrims had been on the deck, and a big wave had washed him into the sea. As he was swept overboard, however, he somehow grabbed a rope hanging from the ship. He managed to hold on until the sailors could pull him up.

The rain caused other problems as well. Flooding damaged the food supply, leaving little to eat. Most meals were salt pork and hard, dry biscuits called *hardtack*. Usually, the biscuits were crawling with bugs.

There were some bright moments, however, on the *Mayflower*. One was the birth of a baby. His proud parents named him Oceanus.

For all on board, however, the brightest moment was the sight of land on November 21, 1620. The Pilgrims had been at sea for 66 days! They knelt in prayer to give thanks for their safe crossing. And they asked God to protect them in their new world.

Name _____ Date _____

A Dangerous Crossing

Choose the best answer and mark the letter of your choice.

1. What is this article mostly about?

   A. the Pilgrims' beliefs
   B. storms at sea
   C. sailing on the *Mayflower*
   D. crowded ships

2. In this article, the word *expedition* means

   F. a dangerous weather condition.
   G. an adventure paid for by the government.
   H. an exploration of the ocean floor.
   J. a long and dangerous trip.

3. The *Mayflower* was overcrowded because

   A. there were too many sailors.
   B. the Pilgrims took too many trunks.
   C. the captain sold extra tickets to make money.
   D. the Pilgrims had to use one ship instead of two.

4. Which of these is a fact presented in the article?

   F. Weather was not a problem during the trip.
   G. Bad weather caused serious problems during the trip.
   H. The *Mayflower* was not fit to sail in bad weather.
   J. The captain was not used to sailing in bad weather.

5. In this article, the word *seasick* means

   A. sickened by a ship's movement.
   B. tired of a sea journey.
   C. sick of traveling by ship.
   D. frightened of the sea.

6. In this article, the word *hardtack* means

   F. dried pork.
   G. hard, dry biscuits.
   H. any food that has bugs in it.
   J. stale cake.

7. The Pilgrims finally saw land

   A. in October.
   B. on September 16, 1620.
   C. after 60 days of being at sea.
   D. on November 21, 1620.

8. The article gives you enough information to conclude that

   F. the journey would have been easier with fewer sailors.
   G. the ship was not too crowded for the number of passengers.
   H. the expedition would have been easier with two ships.
   J. the trip should not have been made at all.

UNIT 2
The Story of Chocolate

A·B·C *L*ESSON *P*LANNER

1. *A*ccess
- **READING STRATEGY:** Use the Anticipation Guide on page 14 before having small groups of students read the article. Write the statements on the board, or use the sheet as a copying master. Invite students to tell whether they agree or disagree with each statement. They can write their responses in their journals or learning logs. Do not expect students to know the answers. This activity is designed to help build interest, activate prior knowledge, and set purposes for reading.

2. *B*uild
- Have students read the article, or read it aloud to them.
- As students read or after they finish reading the article, they may change their opinions about the statements. If they do, have them discuss why they revised their opinions, and have them state what they learned from their reading that allowed them to confirm or revise their opinions.

3. *C*lose
- Have students complete the standardized-test-format questions after they read the article. (An item analysis that identifies the test objectives covered by each question, as well as an answer key, can be found on page 65.)
- **LANGUAGE ARTS ACTIVITY:** Have students look through cookbooks for information about chocolate and cocoa. Then have them find recipes for making different types of foods or drinks with cocoa or chocolate. Students can share their recipes.

Name _____ Date _____

The Story of Chocolate
Anticipation Guide

Check One

	Agree	Disagree
1. The Aztecs learned about chocolate from Cortés.		
2. Chocolate is made from cocoa beans.		
3. Cortés brought chocolate to Spain.		
4. Hot chocolate was never very popular in Europe.		
5. Chocolate candy is eaten all over the world.		

The Story of Chocolate

When Cortés arrived in Tenochtitlán, Motecuhzoma welcomed him with a great feast. After the meal a chocolate drink was served in gold cups. It was cold and bitter and had a peppery taste. Cortés didn't like it much, but he was fascinated by the fuss the Aztecs made over it.

What Cortés didn't know, but would soon find out, was that the Aztecs believed chocolate was a gift from the god Quetzalcoatl. Those who drank it were supposed to gain wisdom and strength. For that reason, only rulers and soldiers were allowed to have it. Motecuhzoma drank 50 cups of it a day!

The Aztecs made chocolate from cocoa beans, just as we do today. But for the Aztecs, cocoa beans were important for another reason. The Aztecs used them as money. A rabbit, for example, cost 10 cocoa beans, while a slave cost 100.

It didn't take long for Cortés to figure out that he could make money by growing and selling cocoa beans. He had them planted all over Central America and later in Africa. He also took some with him when he went home to Spain.

The Spanish didn't like chocolate at first. Then they added sugar to the drink. After that, it became so popular that the Spanish tried to keep it a secret. They succeeded for almost 100 years. But, little by little, word got out.

Over the years members of Spain's royal family married *monarchs* from other European countries. The kings and queens shared the sweet secret among themselves. By the middle of the seventeenth century, hot chocolate had become Europe's favorite drink. And chocolate houses replaced coffee shops as a popular place for social gatherings and business meetings.

It took another 200 years, however, for someone to figure out that if chocolate was so good to drink, it would also be good to eat. The British claim credit for that discovery, and they deserve it. It was the British firm of Fry & Sons that made the first "eating chocolate" in 1847.

The rest is history. Chocolate candy seemed to satisfy the sweet tooth as no other candy could. It became a best-seller in Britain and soon spread to the rest of the world. Today, there are chocolate fans everywhere!

Name _____ Date _____

The Story of Chocolate

Choose the best answer and mark the letter of your choice.

1. What is this article mostly about?
   A. how chocolate spread around the world
   B. how chocolate is created from cocoa beans
   C. what makes chocolate popular all over the world
   D. Cortés and his first encounter with the Aztecs

2. What did the Aztecs believe chocolate would give them?
   F. new rulers
   G. wisdom and strength
   H. long life
   J. wealth and power

3. According to the article, which of these happened first?
   A. Cortés brought cocoa beans to Spain.
   B. Cortés learned about chocolate from the Aztecs.
   C. The Spanish added sugar to chocolate.
   D. Chocolate became popular in Europe.

4. Cortés planted cocoa beans because
   F. he had grown to like the taste of chocolate.
   G. the king of Spain requested it.
   H. he wanted to become a farmer.
   J. he thought he could make money by selling the beans.

5. In this article, the word *monarchs* means
   A. chocolate makers.
   B. rich people.
   C. kings and queens.
   D. lords and ladies.

6. The first "eating chocolate" was made
   F. by the Aztecs.
   G. by Cortés.
   H. by the British.
   J. by the Spanish.

7. Which of these is a fact presented in the article?
   A. Chocolate is the world's oldest candy.
   B. Everyone likes chocolate.
   C. Chocolate is better to eat than to drink.
   D. Chocolate is a popular candy.

8. The article gives you enough information to predict that chocolate will probably
   F. be cheaper in the future.
   G. continue to be popular in the future.
   H. be more expensive in the future.
   J. taste better in the future.

16 • Unit 2

UNIT 3
Barn Raising

A·B·C *L*ESSON *P*LANNER

1. *A*ccess

- **READING STRATEGY:** Use the Word Splash on page 18 to help students make predictions about the article. Write the words on the board, or use the sheet as a copying master. Invite students to predict how each word or phrase relates to barn raisings. Students can write their predictions in their journals or learning logs. Do not expect students to know the answers. This activity is designed to help build interest, activate prior knowledge, and set purposes for reading.

2. *B*uild

- Have students read the article, or read it aloud to them.
- As students read or after they finish reading the article, they may change their Word Splash predictions. Have them identify the predictions that were correct, and have them state what they have learned from reading the article.

3. *C*lose

- Have students complete the standardized-test-format questions after they read the article. (An item analysis that identifies the test objectives covered by each question, as well as an answer key, can be found on page 66.)
- **MATHEMATICS ACTIVITY:** Have students find pictures of frontier barns and then design one. Students can try different measurements for their barn and then create word problems involving the measurements.

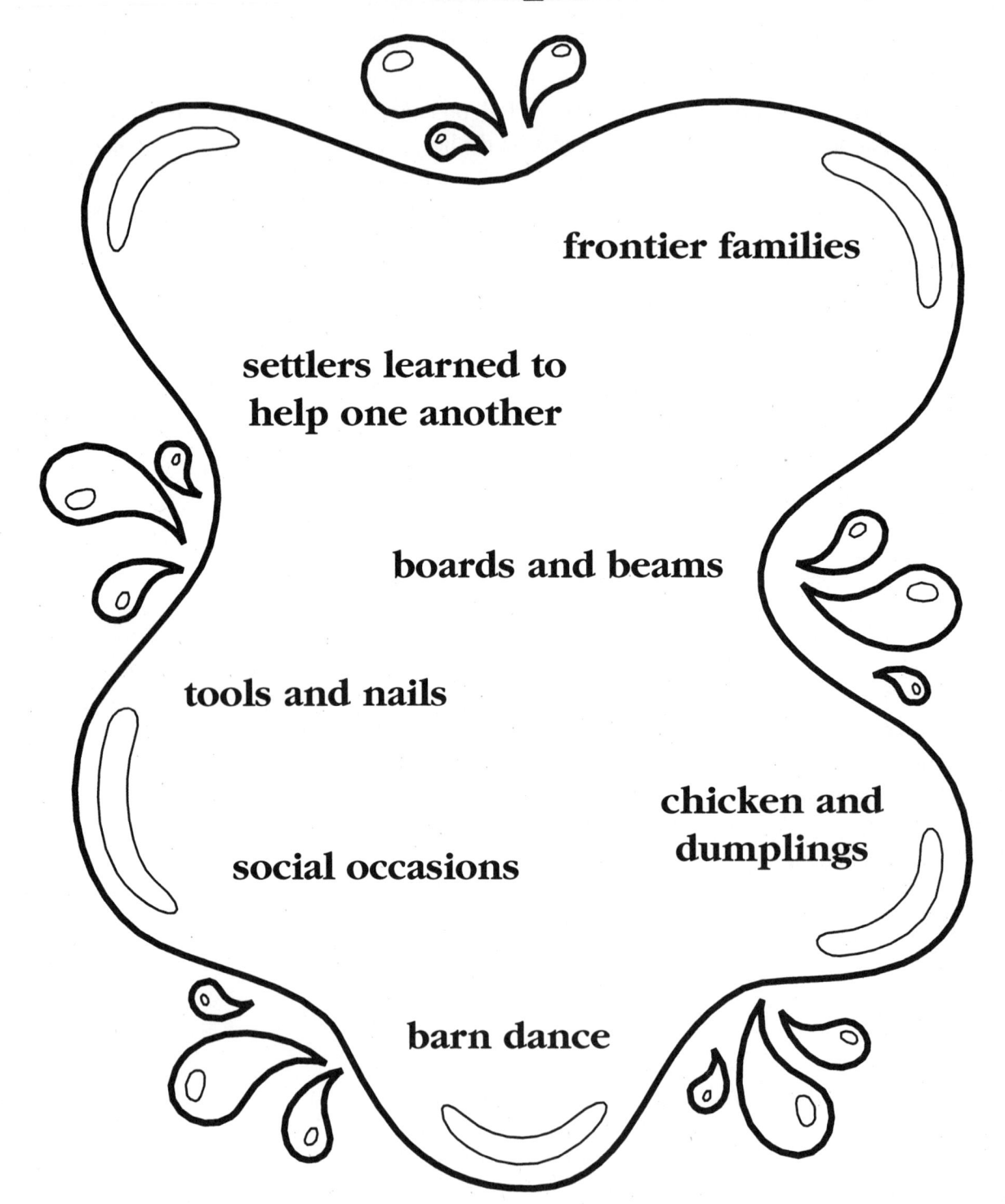

Name _____ Date _____

Barn Raising
Word Splash

frontier families

settlers learned to
help one another

boards and beams

tools and nails

chicken and
dumplings

social occasions

barn dance

18 • Unit 3

BARN RAISING

Life was hard for people who lived on the *frontier*. On the western border of settlement, there was never enough time for all the work that had to be done. The settlers had to learn to help one another. Working together made a job go faster. It also made the job more fun. A barn raising was one of the ways frontier families had fun while getting work done.

At a barn raising neighbors came from miles around to help a family build a barn. The men worked in teams to chop down trees and cut them into boards and *beams*. The boards were used for the floor of the barn. The beams were used for the frame. Once the frame was up, the owner could finish the barn alone.

Putting the frame in place was a difficult process. First, the beams had to be laid out on the ground in exactly the right position. Next, they had to be cut to the correct size and shape. Then the beams had to be nailed together to make the frame. After that the entire frame had to be raised. All the men in the group worked together on that job, which took all their strength.

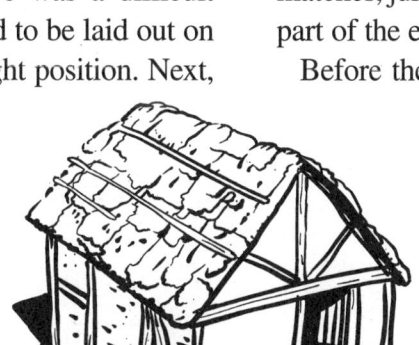

While the building was going on, the children carried tools and nails to the workers. They also took them drinks, usually apple cider or lemonade. Meanwhile, the women were busy preparing food for a hearty meal.

Social occasions like barn raisings gave women a chance to show off their cooking skills. Some made soups and stews, while others cooked dishes such as chicken and dumplings. Still others brought bacon, sausages, and hams. Immigrant women often made dishes from their native lands. All the women had homemade bread, pies, cakes, and cookies to add to the table.

After the meal and a rest, it was time for fun. Both children and adults enjoyed wrestling matches, jumping contests, and races. The best part of the evening was the barn dance.

Before the dancing began, people scattered kernels of corn across the barn floor. Then, as everyone danced, they stepped on the corn, pressing oil out of the kernels. The oil polished the rough floorboards. In addition to being fun, the barn dance served a useful purpose.

Unit 3 • 19

Name _____ Date _____

Barn Raising

Choose the best answer and mark the letter of your choice.

1. What is the main idea of this article?
    A. Frontier families did not know how to build barns.
    B. Frontier families worked together and had fun together at barn raisings.
    C. Frontier families needed barns.
    D. Frontier families enjoyed barn dances.

2. In this article, the word *frontier* means
    F. a western colony.
    G. a distant neighborhood.
    H. a place where people helped each other.
    J. the western border of settlement.

3. In this article, the word *beams* means
    A. boards used for floors.
    B. frames for barns.
    C. tools for workers.
    D. rays of light.

4. What happens first in the frame-making process?
    F. The beams are laid on the ground in the right position.
    G. The beams are cut to the correct size and shape.
    H. The beams are nailed together.
    J. The frame is raised.

5. During a barn raising, children helped by
    A. carrying supplies and drinks.
    B. making lemonade.
    C. preparing food.
    D. nailing boards together.

6. Why did the women enjoy barn raisings?
    F. They could show off their sewing skills.
    G. They could help the men build the barn.
    H. They could show off their cooking skills.
    J. They could spend the day resting.

7. By stepping on corn kernels, dancers at a barn dance helped
    A. paint the barn floor.
    B. polish the barn floor.
    C. clean the barn floor.
    D. make the dance more fun.

8. The article gives you enough information to conclude that
    F. frontier men always worked in teams.
    G. barn raisings were the only social events on the frontier.
    H. people who did not help each other could not survive.
    J. working together made life easier and more enjoyable for frontier people.

UNIT 3
School Days

A·B·C *Lesson Planner*

1. *Access*

- **READING STRATEGY:** Use the Anticipation Guide on page 22 before having small groups of students read the article. Write the statements on the board, or use the sheet as a copying master. Invite students to tell whether they agree or disagree with each statement. They can write their responses in their journals or learning logs. Do not expect students to know the answers. This activity is designed to help build interest, activate prior knowledge, and set purposes for reading.

2. *Build*

- Have students read the article, or read it aloud to them.
- As students read or after they finish reading the article, they may change their opinions about the statements. If they do, have them discuss why they revised their opinions, and have them state what they learned from their reading that allowed them to confirm or revise their opinions.

3. *Close*

- Have students complete the standardized-test-format questions after they read the article. (An item analysis that identifies the test objectives covered by each question, as well as an answer key, can be found on page 66.)
- **LANGUAGE ARTS ACTIVITY:** Have students write a rhyme that could be used to help them remember a lesson they are learning in school. Students may wish to make a book of rhyming lessons.

Name _____ Date _____

School Days
Anticipation Guide

Check One

	Agree	Disagree
1. Puritan boys and girls were taught to read.		
2. All Puritan children went to public schools.		
3. Boys wrote their lessons on sheets of birchbark.		
4. Children were never punished in colonial schools.		
5. Lessons were often written in rhyme.		

School Days

The Puritans believed that everyone should read the Bible. That is why they sent their children to school to learn to read. Young boys and girls went to schools run by women in their homes. These schools were called dame schools. Colonial people used the word *dame* the way we use the word *Mrs.* today.

The children learned to read from a one-page book. Actually, it wasn't really a book at all. It was a sheet of paper printed with the alphabet, numbers, and the Lord's Prayer. The paper was pasted to a paddle-shaped piece of wood and covered with a thin layer of clear animal horn. For that reason, it was called a *hornbook*.

A child who could read and write everything on the hornbook was ready to move on. For a girl that meant learning *housekeeping* skills at home. For a boy it meant going to public school.

Massachusetts set up the first public school system in the colonies. Every town with 50 families or more had to build a school for boys. The law said boys had to attend.

The school was usually a large, unheated room, which was freezing cold in winter. The boys studied Latin, Greek, and geography. They also studied reading, writing, and arithmetic. Most of the time they recited their lessons out loud. Paper was so *scarce* in the colonies that it could not be used for schoolwork. Instead of using paper, the boys wrote on smooth, white bark, which they peeled from birch trees.

Most of the children worked hard at school. A boy who didn't learn his lessons was called a *dunce*. He had to stand in a corner, wearing a pointed hat called a *dunce cap*. There were other kinds of punishments in colonial schools as well.

Lessons were often written in rhyme to help children remember them. A common rhyme helped children remember the number of days in each month. We still use that rhyme today. Do you know it?

Name _____ Date _____

School Days

Choose the best answer and mark the letter of your choice.

1. What is this article mostly about?

    A. colonial children
    B. Puritans
    C. colonial schools
    D. colonial books

2. The Puritans believed that everyone should read the Bible, so they

    F. sent children to school to learn to read.
    G. gave everyone Bibles.
    H. sent children to church to learn to read.
    J. had Bible-reading classes every day.

3. In this article, the word *hornbook* means

    A. Bible verse.
    B. one-page book.
    C. birchbark tablet.
    D. book of rhymes.

4. In this article, the word *housekeeping* means

    F. staying at home.
    G. owning a house.
    H. learning skills.
    J. taking care of a house.

5. Massachusetts was the first colony to

    A. use hornbooks.
    B. set up a public school system.
    C. have dame schools.
    D. have towns with more than 50 families.

6. What did a child do after he or she knew everything on the hornbook?

    F. A girl went to public school and a boy worked on the farm.
    G. Both a boy and a girl went to public school.
    H. A girl learned housekeeping and a boy went to public school.
    J. Both a boy and a girl worked at home.

7. In this article, the word *scarce* means

    A. expensive.
    B. badly made.
    C. inexpensive.
    D. not plentiful.

8. The article gives you enough information to generalize that in colonial times

    F. boys had more education than girls.
    G. girls learned faster than boys.
    H. girls did not need an education.
    J. education was not important for boys or girls.

UNIT 4
Benjamin Franklin: Writer, Scientist, Statesman

A·B·C Lesson Planner

1. Access

- **READING STRATEGY:** Use the Anticipation Guide on page 26 before having small groups of students read the article. Write the statements on the board, or use the sheet as a copying master. Invite students to tell whether they agree or disagree with each statement. They can write their responses in their journals or learning logs. Do not expect students to know the answers. This activity is designed to help build interest, activate prior knowledge, and set purposes for reading.

2. Build

- Have students read the article, or read it aloud to them.
- As students read or after they finish reading the article, they may change their opinions about the statements. If they do, have them discuss why they revised their opinions, and have them state what they learned from their reading that allowed them to confirm or revise their opinions.

3. Close

- Have students complete the standardized-test-format questions after they read the article. (An item analysis that identifies the test objectives covered by each question, as well as an answer key, can be found on page 66.)
- **SCIENCE ACTIVITY:** Have students use reference materials to conduct research on electricity—how it is created, what it is used for, and how it is stored. Invite students to share their findings with the class.

Name _____ Date _____

Benjamin Franklin: Writer, Scientist, Statesman
Anticipation Guide

Check One

	Agree	Disagree
1. Benjamin Franklin created a plan for the colonies called the "Plan of Union."		
2. Franklin's favorite subject was history.		
3. *Poor Richard's Almanack* contained clever sayings.		
4. In 1776 Franklin sailed to France to try to get help for the colonies.		
5. Franklin fought in the War of 1812.		

BENJAMIN FRANKLIN:
Writer, Scientist, Statesman

During the French and Indian War, Benjamin Franklin created a bold new plan for the colonies. He proposed that they join together for "defense and other general purposes." His "Plan of Union" was a good idea, but it was ahead of its time. The colonies were not yet ready to unite. However, their leaders continued to ask Franklin for advice. After all, he was considered one of the wisest men in the American colonies.

How did Franklin earn such a reputation? He did it by serving his country in many ways: as a writer, a scientist, and a statesman.

When he was only 26, Franklin wrote the first edition of *Poor Richard's Almanack*. It included a calendar, weather forecasts, and other information that most almanacs contain. It also had something extra: clever sayings that gave useful advice in a humorous way. The sayings became very popular and *Poor Richard's Almanack* soon became the most popular book in the colonies.

Franklin published his almanacs each year for 25 years. The money the sale of almanacs made let him devote his time to his favorite subject: science.

Franklin had always loved to experiment. As a child he discovered that if he flew a kite while swimming, it would pull him through the water. Years later he turned his attention to more practical inventions such as the Franklin stove. The Franklin stove gave off more heat than a fireplace but used less wood. However, it was not until his experiment with electricity in 1752 that Franklin became known worldwide.

Franklin used his fame to help his country as a *statesman* during the American Revolution. Late in 1776 he sailed to France seeking support for the colonies.

The French gave Franklin a warm welcome. His popularity helped Franklin convince the French to supply the colonists with soldiers and weapons to help fight the British. Many historians believe that the American Patriots would have lost the Revolution without France's help.

After the war Franklin helped write the peace *treaty* between Britain and the United States. This agreement gave the new country the right to govern itself. The United States had gained its *independence* from Britain. And Benjamin Franklin had served his country once again.

Name _____ Date _____

Benjamin Franklin: Writer, Scientist, Statesman

Choose the best answer and mark the letter of your choice.

1. Which of these is the best summary of this article?
   A. Benjamin Franklin was a famous writer.
   B. Benjamin Franklin believed that the colonies should unite.
   C. Benjamin Franklin served his country in many ways.
   D. Benjamin Franklin was a great scientist.

2. The article gives you enough information to conclude that Franklin had a sense of humor because he
   F. enjoyed telling jokes.
   G. wrote jokes in his almanacs.
   H. wrote humorous sayings in his almanacs.
   J. wrote humorous stories.

3. Benjamin Franklin became known worldwide because of
   A. his almanacs.
   B. his experiment with electricity.
   C. his Franklin stove.
   D. his visit to France.

4. In this article, the word *statesman* means
   F. a leader who represents his government in other countries.
   G. a person who makes statements.
   H. a writer of almanacs.
   J. a leader in business.

5. Franklin's trip to France resulted in
   A. French aid to the colonies.
   B. a French version of his almanac.
   C. French settlers coming to the United States.
   D. a meeting with French scientists.

6. Without France's help during the Revolution, the American Patriots might have
   F. asked Britain for help.
   G. become part of France.
   H. been conquered by Spain.
   J. lost the war.

7. In this article, the word *treaty* means
   A. a plan of action.
   B. an agreement between countries.
   C. a new state law.
   D. an important report.

8. In this article, the word *independence* means
   F. the ability to survive.
   G. the freedom to govern on one's own.
   H. the freedom to travel anywhere in the world.
   J. the need for a treaty.

UNIT 4
The Spirit of 1776

A·B·C LESSON PLANNER

1. Access

- **READING STRATEGY:** Use the Word Splash on page 30 to help students make predictions about the article. Write the words on the board, or use the sheet as a copying master. Invite students to predict how each word or phrase relates to the events of 1776. Students can write their predictions in their journals or learning logs. Do not expect students to know the answers. This activity is designed to help build interest, activate prior knowledge, and set purposes for reading.

2. Build

- Have students read the article, or read it aloud to them.
- As students read or after they finish reading the article, they may change their Word Splash predictions. Have them identify the predictions that were correct, and have them state what they have learned from reading the article.

3. Close

- Have students complete the standardized-test-format questions after they read the article. (An item analysis that identifies the test objectives covered by each question, as well as an answer key, can be found on page 66.)
- **LANGUAGE ARTS ACTIVITY:** Have students make a list of basic human rights. Students can use the Declaration of Independence as a basis for their lists and can add other rights that people in this and the next century may need to have protected.

Name _____ Date _____

The Spirit of 1776
Word Splash

"We hold these Truths to be self-evident."

life and liberty

signatures

traitor

King George

unjust rule

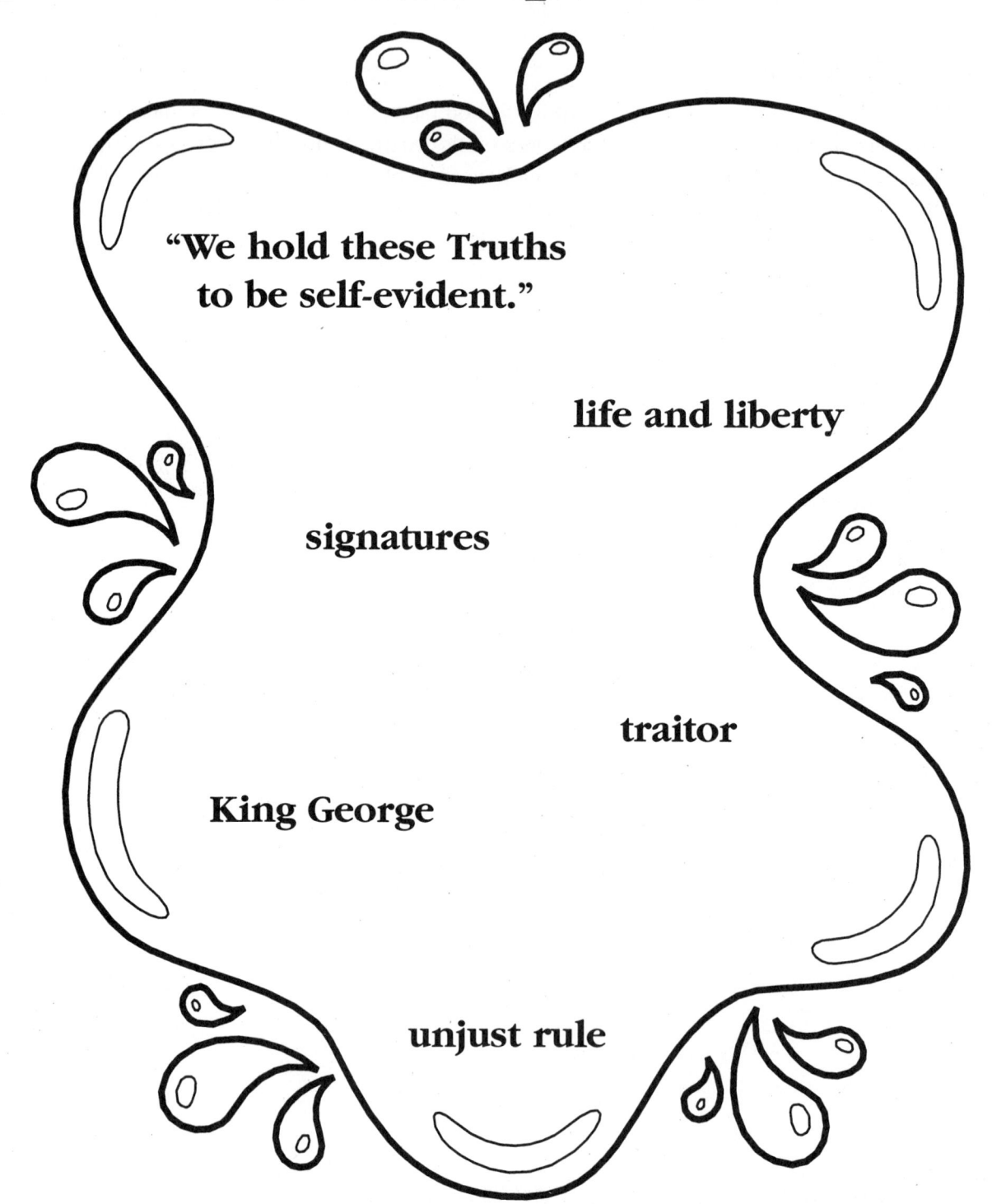

30 • Unit 4

The Spirit of 1776

Of all the signatures on the Declaration of Independence, John Hancock's stands out. Not only is his name first, it is also larger than the others. It is said that Hancock wrote his name in large letters so King George wouldn't have to put on his glasses to see it. Whether this is true, no one can say for sure. We do know that it took great courage for Hancock to sign the Declaration of Independence. King George had already called him a traitor and offered a reward for his capture.

The other signers of the Declaration of Independence also were in danger. If the colonies lost the war, the British would accuse them of working against the government. This would be an act of treason, and such acts of *treason* could be punished by death. Benjamin Franklin tried to joke about this when it was his turn to sign. "We must all hang together," he said, "or we shall all hang separately."

The signers of the Declaration of Independence were willing to risk their lives because they believed in the principles stated in that document. When Thomas Jefferson wrote the words, "We hold these Truths to be self-evident, that all Men are created equal, that they are endowed by their Creator with certain unalienable Rights, that among these are Life, Liberty, and the Pursuit of Happiness," the ideas were not new. However, the Declaration of Independence was the first step toward forming a government based on those beliefs. Since 1776 it has inspired people around the world to seek this kind of government for themselves.

For example, in 1789 the people of France rebelled against the unjust rule of their king. In time they created a more democratic government based, in part, on the ideals expressed in the Declaration of Independence. In the early 1800s many Latin American colonies rebelled against Spanish rule. Inspired by the Declaration of Independence, they fought for and won the right to *self-government*.

Today the spirit of the Declaration of Independence lives on in another important document. These words are from the Universal Declaration of Human Rights, issued by the United Nations soon after it was formed: "All human beings are born free and equal in dignity and rights. Everyone is entitled to all the rights and freedoms set forth in this Declaration.... Everyone has the right to life, liberty and security of person." The spirit of 1776 lives on today.

Name _____ Date _____

The Spirit of 1776

Choose the best answer and mark the letter of your choice.

1. What is this article mostly about?
   A. the leaders who signed the Declaration of Independence
   B. the Declaration of Independence and how its spirit lives on
   C. the birth of the United States
   D. independence, equality, and democracy

2. In this article, the word *treason* means
   F. working against one's own government.
   G. working against any government.
   H. signing a declaration.
   J. working for democracy.

3. What is the main idea of the second paragraph?
   A. King George declared John Hancock a traitor.
   B. To Franklin, signing the Declaration of Independence was a joke.
   C. To the British, signing the Declaration of Independence was an act of treason.
   D. John Hancock feared signing the Declaration of Independence.

4. The leaders who signed the Declaration of Independence
   F. kept their action a secret.
   G. refused to declare war.
   H. sent their families to Britain for safety.
   J. put their lives at risk.

5. *Self-government* is a system of government in which
   A. people make their own laws.
   B. one person makes the laws.
   C. there are no laws.
   D. there are revolutions.

6. According to the article, which of these happened first?
   F. Colonies in Latin America rebelled against Spanish rule.
   G. The French rebelled against their king.
   H. The Declaration of Independence was signed.
   J. The Universal Declaration of Human Rights was issued.

7. The Universal Declaration of Human Rights is
   A. another name for the Declaration of Independence.
   B. a statement issued by the United Nations.
   C. a statement about the universe.
   D. a list of international laws.

8. The article gives you enough information to conclude that
   F. the ideas in the Declaration of Independence apply only to the United States.
   G. the ideas in the Declaration of Independence do not apply today.
   H. the Declaration of Independence is the most important document in the world.
   J. the ideas in the Declaration of Independence apply to people all over the world.

32 • Unit 4

UNIT 5
Father of the Constitution

A·B·C *L*ESSON *P*LANNER

1. *A*ccess

- **READING STRATEGY:** Use the Anticipation Guide on page 34 before having small groups of students read the article. Write the statements on the board, or use the sheet as a copying master. Invite students to tell whether they agree or disagree with each statement. They can write their responses in their journals or learning logs. Do not expect students to know the answers. This activity is designed to help build interest, activate prior knowledge, and set purposes for reading.

2. *B*uild

- Have students read the article, or read it aloud to them.
- As students read or after they finish reading the article, they may change their opinions about the statements. If they do, have them discuss why they revised their opinions, and have them state what they learned from their reading that allowed them to confirm or revise their opinions.

3. *C*lose

- Have students complete the standardized-test-format questions after they read the article. (An item analysis that identifies the test objectives covered by each question, as well as an answer key, can be found on page 67.)
- **MATHEMATICS ACTIVITY:** Have students create a time line of significant events associated with drafting the Constitution. Then invite students to create addition and subtraction problems using some of the dates.

Name _____ Date _____

Father of the Constitution
Anticipation Guide

Check One

	Agree	Disagree
1. Everything that happened at the Constitutional Convention was reported in the newspapers.		
2. James Madison took notes on the meetings.		
3. Madison wanted to try to fix the Articles of Confederation.		
4. The delegates voted against Madison's idea for a three-part government.		
5. The Constitution of the United States was based on many of Madison's ideas.		

Father of the Constitution

The delegates to the Constitutional Convention spent almost four months in a hot, stuffy room. The doors were closed and the windows were nailed shut, even during the hot summer months of July and August. The delegates could have used some fresh air, but privacy was more important. They wanted to be able to speak freely, without worrying about public opinion. Everything that happened in that room was a closely guarded secret. How is it, then, that we know exactly what went on? We have James Madison to thank for that.

Madison took notes on everything that was said and done during the meetings. At the end of each day, he went back to his room and wrote up his notes. It was very tiring work. Sometimes the speeches lasted for hours, and Madison would end up writing more than 20 pages in a single night. "This was a task that nearly killed me," he later said. But it was worth the effort. Because of Madison, we have a complete record of what went on at the Constitutional Convention. That is one reason he is known as the Father of the Constitution. There is another reason as well.

When James Madison arrived at the convention, he was already convinced that a new plan of government was needed—a plan that would make the national government stronger than the states. He had just such a plan.

At the first meeting, on May 25, Madison did two things. He chose a chair up front so that he would not miss a word. He also made sure that his plan was presented right away. He did not want the delegates to waste valuable time trying to fix the Articles of Confederation.

Madison wanted a three-part government with a legislative branch, an executive branch, and a judicial branch. This would create a government in which no one branch would have more power than another. The delegates liked this idea but they disagreed with some of his other ideas. They would have to *compromise* on still others. So Madison gave up some ideas to get what he really wanted. By May 30, however, they had heard enough to make a major decision. They decided not to try to fix the Articles of Confederation. Instead, they would write a new *constitution*. This new plan of government would be based on many of Madison's ideas. That is a second reason Madison is known as the Father of the Constitution.

Name _____ Date _____

Father of the Constitution

Choose the best answer and mark the letter of your choice.

1. Which of these is the best summary for this article?
   A. The United States needed a new plan for a government.
   B. The delegates to the Constitutional Convention wrote the Constitution in a hot, stuffy room.
   C. Madison convinced people to revise the Articles of Confederation.
   D. Madison's ideas and his records of the Constitutional Convention made him the Father of the Constitution.

2. As a result of the notes that James Madison took,
   F. we know what happened at the Constitutional Convention.
   G. the doors were closed and the windows were nailed shut.
   H. he was chosen president.
   J. the Constitution was written.

3. Madison came up with a new plan of government
   A. after he arrived at the convention.
   B. during the convention.
   C. before the opening of the convention.
   D. on May 25.

4. The delegates agreed with
   F. all of Madison's ideas.
   G. Madison's idea for a three-part government.
   H. the notes Madison took.
   J. the idea of fixing the Articles of Confederation.

5. According to the article, how would a three-part government work?
   A. The legislative branch would be the most powerful.
   B. The executive branch would be the most powerful.
   C. The judicial branch would be the most powerful.
   D. No one branch would have more power than another.

6. In this article, the word *compromise* means
   F. agreed with all ideas.
   G. gave up some ideas to reach agreement on other ideas.
   H. did not agree with any ideas.
   J. accepted some ideas.

7. In this article, the word *constitution* means
   A. a new government.
   B. a compromise.
   C. an amendment.
   D. a plan of government.

8. The article gives you enough information to conclude that
   F. Madison was responsible for a new plan of government.
   G. Many of the delegates had the same ideas as Madison.
   H. Madison did not like the Articles of Confederation.
   J. Madison's ideas were not accepted.

UNIT 5
Abigail Adams, A Woman Ahead of Her Time

A·B·C Lesson Planner

1. Access

- **READING STRATEGY:** Use the Word Splash on page 38 to help students make predictions about the article. Write the words on the board, or use the sheet as a copying master. Invite students to predict how each word or phrase relates to Abigail Adams. Students can write their predictions in their journals or learning logs. Do not expect students to know the answers. This activity is designed to help build interest, activate prior knowledge, and set purposes for reading.

2. Build

- Have students read the article, or read it aloud to them.
- As students read or after they finish reading the article, they may change their Word Splash predictions. Have them identify the predictions that were correct, and have them state what they have learned from reading the article.

3. Close

- Have students complete the standardized-test-format questions after they read the article. (An item analysis that identifies the test objectives covered by each question, as well as an answer key, can be found on page 67.)
- **LANGUAGE ARTS ACTIVITY:** Have students write a letter to the editor explaining how Abigail Adams was a woman who was ahead of her time. Invite students to provide reasons from the article to support their statements.

Name _____ Date _____

Abigail Adams, A Woman Ahead of Her Time
Word Splash

women and men are equal

spoke her mind

ahead of her time

First Lady

power of the press

new capital city

slave labor

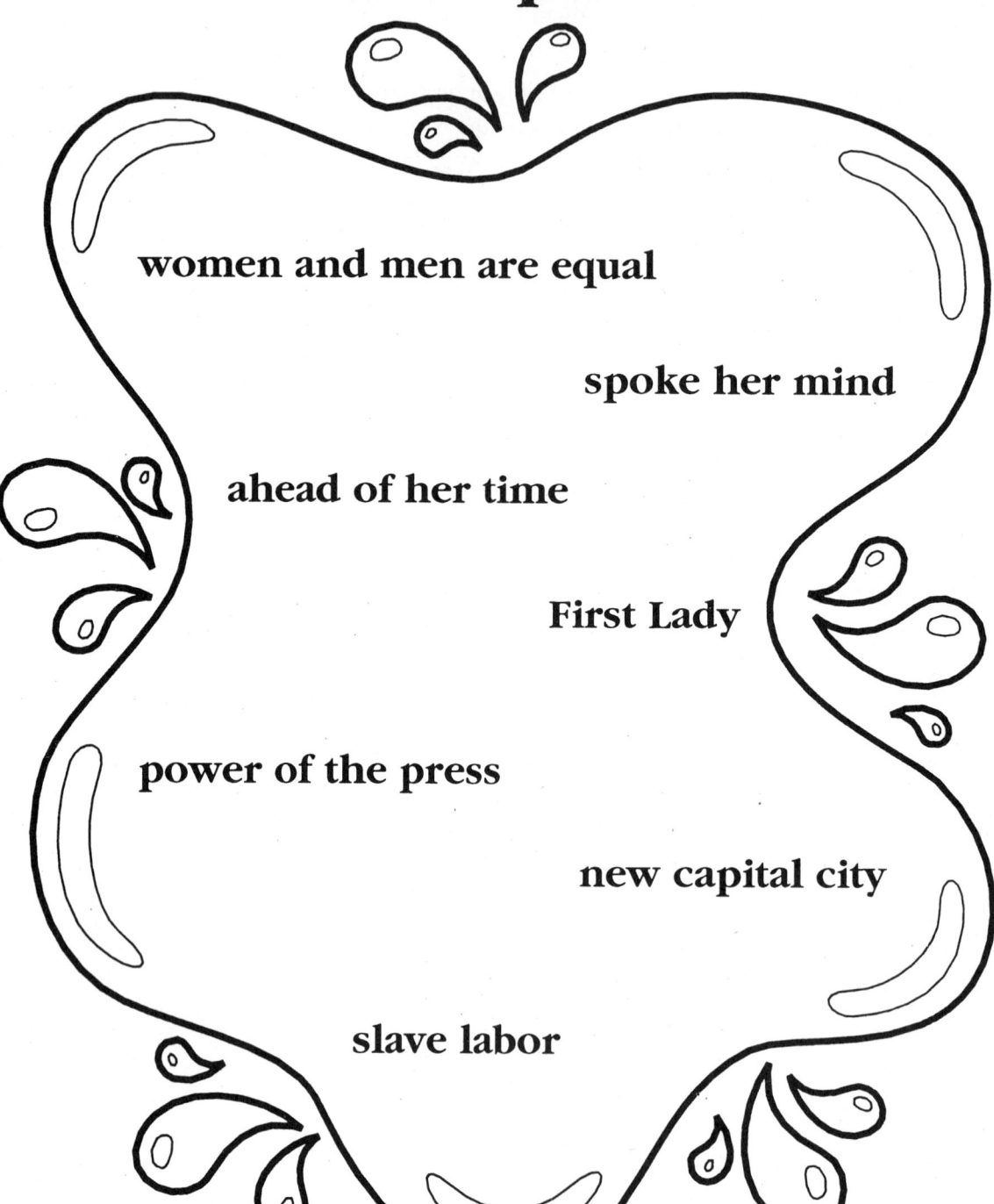

38 • Unit 5

Abigail Adams, A Woman Ahead of Her Time

Abigail Adams lived in a society in which women could not vote, hold office, or attend college. Formal education was actually considered a disadvantage for a woman. It might make her think she knew as much as her husband!

Abigail Adams didn't see things that way. She thought that women and men should be treated as equals. She made a point of speaking up for what she believed. Sometimes, though, even Abigail Adams had to admit that being *outspoken* could cause problems.

When her husband, John Adams, ran for President in 1796, Abigail Adams worried about becoming *First Lady*. As the President's wife she would have to keep her opinions to herself. She was not sure she could do that.

She was soon put to the test. In 1797 John Adams was elected President. Soon after, Abigail Adams discovered the power of the press.

The newspapers reported what the First Lady said and did. They always seemed to find something to criticize. Some said Abigail Adams spent too much money. Others accused her of being cheap. The most hurtful charge was that she influenced her husband's political decisions.

After three years of being misquoted and misunderstood, Abigail Adams learned to choose her words with care. When she and her husband moved to the new capital city, she praised the President's House, saying that it was "built for ages to come." She decided not to point out that it was not quite ready to live in.

In fact, the house was still being built when Abigail and John moved in. It was cold, dark, and damp, even with fires burning in all 13 of its fireplaces. There wasn't even a place to dry the laundry. The family ended up hanging a clothesline across the conference room. In its unfinished condition, the room was good for little else, Abigail Adams told her sister Mary.

What bothered Abigail Adams most about life in Washington was the widespread use of slave labor. She had always believed that slavery was evil. On this subject she spoke her mind. She had learned to give in on minor matters, but she would never compromise on important issues. Abigail Adams was a woman who knew her mind. She was also a woman who was ahead of her time.

Name _____ Date _____

Abigail Adams, A Woman Ahead of Her Time

Choose the best answer and mark the letter of your choice.

1. Which of these is the best summary for this article?
   A. Abigail Adams was the second First Lady.
   B. Abigail Adams spoke out for what she believed in and was a woman ahead of her time.
   C. Abigail Adams was educated.
   D. Abigail Adams was criticized.

2. In this article, the word *outspoken* means
   F. open and honest.
   G. out loud.
   H. well said.
   J. not polite.

3. In this article, the term *First Lady* means
   A. the wife of the President of the United States.
   B. the wife of the first President of the United States.
   C. the first woman to live in the President's House.
   D. the wife of any politician.

4. Abigail Adams worried about becoming First Lady because she
   F. might be unpopular.
   G. would have to move to the new capital.
   H. would have to keep her opinions to herself.
   J. didn't want to be a politician's wife.

5. Which of these newspaper reports upset Abigail Adams the most?
   A. reports that she was cheap
   B. reports that she influenced her husband's political decisions
   C. reports that she spent too much money
   D. reports that she said the President's House was built for ages to come

6. Abigail and John Adams moved to the new capital
   F. when John first became President.
   G. after the President's House was completed.
   H. before John became President.
   J. toward the end of John's presidency.

7. Which of these is a fact presented in the article?
   A. The First Lady can't have opinions.
   B. Abigail Adams spoke out against slavery.
   C. The press reported that Abigail Adams didn't like the President's House.
   D. Women should not have as much education as men.

8. The article gives you enough information to conclude that
   F. Abigail Adams was not upset by the widespread use of slave labor.
   G. The Adams family owned slaves.
   H. Abigail Adams changed her opinion about slavery.
   J. Abigail Adams was upset by the widespread use of slave labor.

UNIT 6
Gold Fever

A·B·C *Lesson Planner*

1. *Access*

- **READING STRATEGY:** Use the Anticipation Guide on page 42 before having small groups of students read the article. Write the statements on the board, or use the sheet as a copying master. Invite students to tell whether they agree or disagree with each statement. They can write their responses in their journals or learning logs. Do not expect students to know the answers. This activity is designed to help build interest, activate prior knowledge, and set purposes for reading.

2. *Build*

- Have students read the article, or read it aloud to them.
- As students read or after they finish reading the article, they may change their opinions about the statements. If they do, have them discuss why they revised their opinions, and have them state what they learned from their reading that allowed them to confirm or revise their opinions.

3. *Close*

- Have students complete the standardized-test-format questions after they read the article. (An item analysis that identifies the test objectives covered by each question, as well as an answer key, can be found on page 67.)
- **MATHEMATICS ACTIVITY:** Have students research the price of an ounce of gold today. Invite students to compare today's price with the price of an ounce during the gold rush. Encourage students to create word problems about gold and its prices.

Name _____ Date _____

Gold Fever
Anticipation Guide

Check One

	Agree	Disagree
1. James Marshall discovered gold at Sutter's Mill.		
2. By 1849 the rush for gold was over.		
3. A boat trip from Massachusetts to California could cost as much as $1,000.		
4. San Francisco was the port closest to the goldfields.		
5. Searching for gold was easy, enjoyable work.		

42 • Unit 6

Harcourt Brace School Publishers

GOLD FEVER

When James Marshall thought he saw a small lump of gold in the river near Sutter's Mill, he couldn't believe his eyes. He reached down and picked the nugget up. "It made my heart thump," Marshall later recalled, "for I was certain it was gold." Although he wanted to keep his discovery a secret, Marshall couldn't resist bragging to his friends. Soon newspapers were spreading the word that there was gold to be found in California. By 1849 there were many more gold seekers on the Oregon Trail than *pioneers* who were traveling west to settle new places.

Travel by sea was much easier than travel by land, but it was also much more expensive. A boat trip from Massachusetts to California, for example, could cost as much as $1,000. Yet many people were willing to pay that. In fact, so many people signed up that shipbuilding companies on the East Coast had to build more ships to keep up with the demand.

When the ships reached California, they docked in San Francisco, the port closest to the goldfields. By the late 1850s, when "gold fever" reached its peak, about 500 ships lay empty in the harbor. Their crews had left and gone off to search for gold. Like most of the forty-niners, they found hard work and disappointment instead.

Searching for gold was boring, backbreaking work. A miner would bend over a stream and scoop up water and dirt in a pan. Then the miner would tilt the pan to separate any pieces of gold from the water and dirt. This process, called *panning,* went on for many hours from morning until night.

On a good day a miner might find a few tiny nuggets of gold. That wasn't much, especially since an ounce of gold was worth only about $16 in today's money.

Few of the gold seekers ever got rich. Most were lucky if they didn't end up in debt. Prices were so high in the mining camps that the miners had trouble just paying for supplies. A single egg could cost up to $3, a pair of boots about $100, and a barrel of flour as much as $400.

There was money to be made in California after all. It was made by the merchants who sold supplies to the miners.

Name _____   Date _____

Gold Fever

Choose the best answer and mark the letter of your choice.

1. What is this article mostly about?
   - A. the state of California
   - B. Sutter's Mill
   - C. trails to the west
   - D. the gold rush

2. The article gives you enough information to conclude that James Marshall's friends
   - F. told other people that he had discovered gold.
   - G. discovered gold with the help of others.
   - H. worked as employees at Sutter's Mill.
   - J. lived on the East Coast.

3. In this article, the word *pioneers* means
   - A. people who are looking for gold.
   - B. merchants who sell goods to miners.
   - C. people who first settle a new place.
   - D. travelers on trips for pleasure.

4. According to the article, when did "gold fever" reach its peak?
   - F. when gold was worth $16 an ounce
   - G. by the late 1850s
   - H. when the miners were panning for gold
   - J. in 1849

5. Ships lay empty in San Francisco harbor because
   - A. passengers left them to search for gold.
   - B. crews left them to search for gold.
   - C. it was expensive to travel by sea.
   - D. they had reached California.

6. In this article, the word *panning* means
   - F. a method of searching for gold.
   - G. a method of selling gold.
   - H. a way to sell supplies.
   - J. a form of travel.

7. Which of these is a fact presented in the article?
   - A. The forty-niners were lucky to get to California.
   - B. Miners were lucky that they already knew how to pan for gold.
   - C. Merchants who sold supplies to the miners made money.
   - D. Many merchants panned for gold.

8. The article gives you enough information to conclude that
   - F. searching for gold was a profitable activity.
   - G. miners worked very hard for little gold.
   - H. miners had enough money to pay for supplies.
   - J. there was a lot of gold in California.

UNIT 6
An American Story

A·B·C Lesson Planner

1. Access

- **READING STRATEGY:** Use the Word Splash on page 46 to help students make predictions about the article. Write the words on the board, or use the sheet as a copying master. Invite students to predict how each word, phrase, or date relates to the flag of the United States. Students can write their predictions in their journals or learning logs. Do not expect students to know the answers. This activity is designed to help build interest, activate prior knowledge, and set purposes for reading.

2. Build

- Have students read the article, or read it aloud to them.
- As students read or after they finish reading the article, they may change their Word Splash predictions. Have them identify the predictions that were correct, and have them state what they have learned from reading the article.

3. Close

- Have students complete the standardized-test-format questions after they read the article. (An item analysis that identifies the test objectives covered by each question, as well as an answer key, can be found on page 67.)
- **ART ACTIVITY:** Have students research the flags of other nations of the world. Invite individual students to create a drawing of one nation's flag and explain its symbols to the class.

Name _____ Date _____

An American Story
Word Splash

symbol

pride

after the state's admission to the Union

June 14, 1777

13 stars and 13 stripes

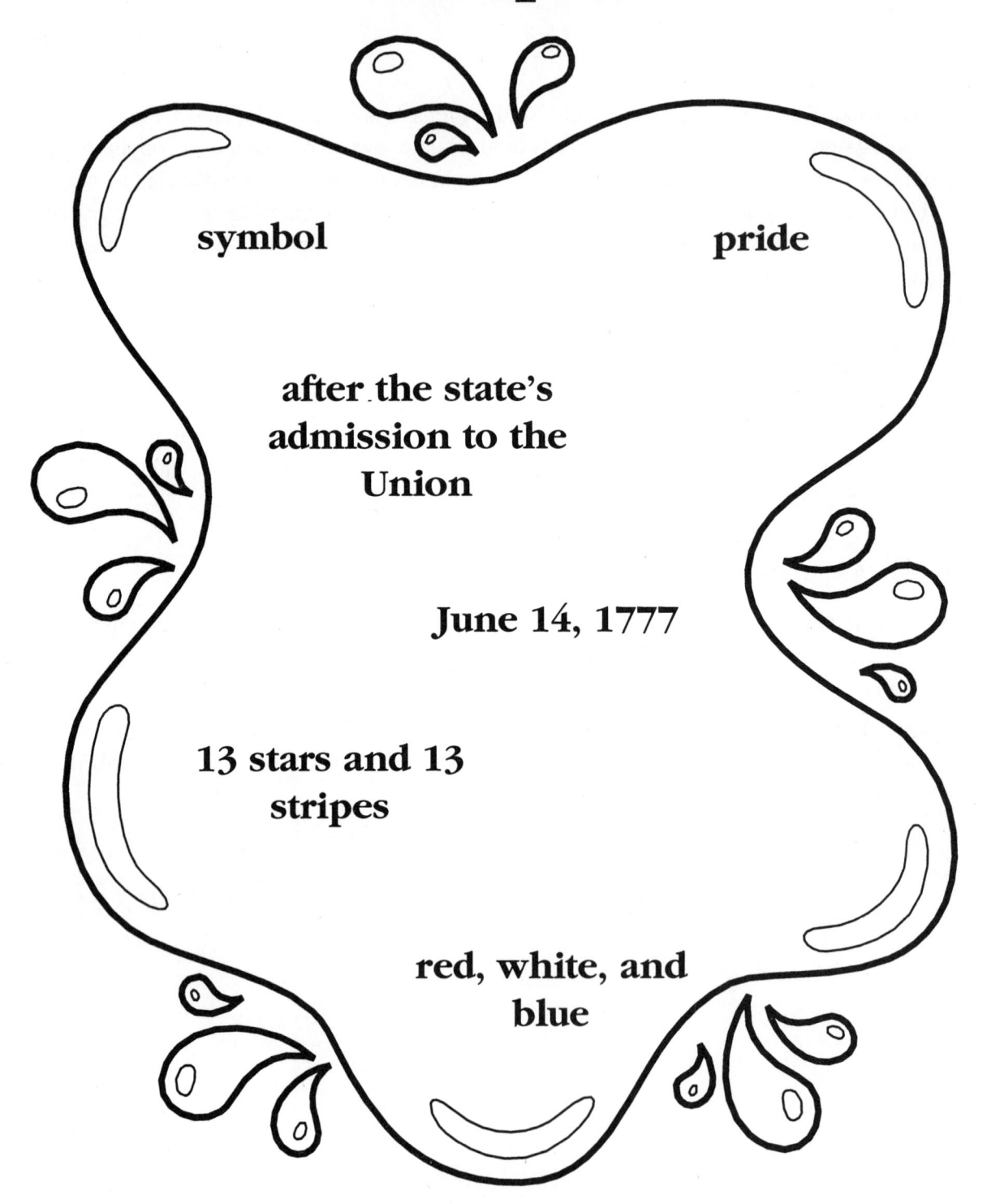

red, white, and blue

An American Story

During his first term of office, President James Monroe expressed a feeling shared by many Americans. He said that the people of the United States were "one great family with a common interest." A wave of *nationalism* was sweeping the land, and pride in the country continued to grow as the nation grew. The story of the American "family" is also the story of the American flag, the oldest and most lasting symbol of this united nation.

On June 14, 1777, Congress approved the design for the first official flag of the United States. The new flag was to have "13 stripes, alternatively red and white," and "13 stars, white in a blue field." The stars and stripes represented the original 13 colonies. Congress also passed a resolution stating that a new star and a new stripe would be added to the flag each time a new state joined the Union.

By 1795 the Union had two new states, Vermont and Kentucky, and the flag had 15 stars and 15 stripes.

In 1814, during the War of 1812, Francis Scott Key wrote "The Star-Spangled Banner." The flag that he saw was the 15-stripe flag. It was flying over Fort McHenry in Maryland.

After the War of 1812, the United States expanded so rapidly that the flag could not keep up with its growth. If a new star and a new stripe were to be added for each state that joined the nation, the flag would be much too large. In 1818 Congress decided to limit the number of stripes to 13 but to add a new star to the flag for each new state. Congress also decided that new stars would be added to the flag on the Fourth of July following a state's admission to the Union.

By 1912 the flag had 48 stars. It stayed that way until Alaska joined the Union in 1959.

Today, the flag of the United States has 50 stars. The last star was added on July 4, 1960, to mark Hawaii's entry into the United States.

Name _____   Date _____

An American Story

Choose the best answer and mark the letter of your choice.

1. Which of these is the best summary for this article?
    A. When James Monroe was President, people were proud of the United States.
    B. The first official American flag had 13 stars and 13 stripes.
    C. The growth of the United States can be seen in its flag.
    D. "The Star-Spangled Banner" is about the flag of the United States.

2. In this article, the word *nationalism* means
    F. growth in population.
    G. expansion to the west.
    H. common interests.
    J. pride in one's country.

3. What did the stars and stripes on the first American flag represent?
    A. the United States Congress
    B. liberty of the people
    C. equality for all
    D. the original 13 colonies

4. According to the article, Vermont and Kentucky became states
    F. after the War of 1812.
    G. before the War of 1812.
    H. during the War of 1812.
    J. during the summer of 1818.

5. In 1818 what caused Congress to limit the number of stripes in the flag to 13?
    A. the fact that many new states were joining the Union
    B. the fact that a new star would be added for each new state
    C. the fact that the War of 1812 had cost so much money
    D. the fact that President Monroe set the number of stripes at 13

6. The article gives you enough information to conclude that the United States had 48 states by 1912 because
    F. the flag had 48 stripes.
    G. the flag had 48 stars.
    H. Alaska was not a state.
    J. a new star was added that year.

7. Which of these is a fact presented in the article?
    A. In 1816 the people of the United States were one great family.
    B. In 1777 many states joined the Union.
    C. In 1777 Congress approved the design for an official U.S. flag.
    D. In 1816 most people felt there were enough states in the Union.

8. If Puerto Rico were to become a state, what would happen to the flag of the United States?
    F. A star would be added.
    G. The flag would stay the same.
    H. A stripe would be added.
    J. A stripe would be removed.

UNIT 7
Balloons in Battle

A·B·C LESSON PLANNER

1. Access

- **READING STRATEGY:** Use the Word Splash on page 50 to help students make predictions about the article. Write the words on the board, or use the sheet as a copying master. Invite students to predict how each word, phrase, or date relates to the flag of the United States. Students can write their predictions in their journals or learning logs. Do not expect students to know the answers. This activity is designed to help build interest, activate prior knowledge, and set purposes for reading.

2. Build

- Have students read the article, or read it aloud to them.
- As students read or after they finish reading the article, they may change their Word Splash predictions. Have them identify which predictions are correct, and have them state what they have learned from reading the article.

3. Close

- Have students complete the standardized-test-format questions after they read the article. (An item analysis that identifies the test objectives covered by each question, as well as an answer key, can be found on page 68.)
- **SCIENCE ACTIVITY:** Have small groups conduct research to find out how gas-filled balloons fly. Then have them find out about helium balloons and uses for balloons. Students can share their findings with other groups.

Name _____ Date _____

Balloons in Battle

Word Splash

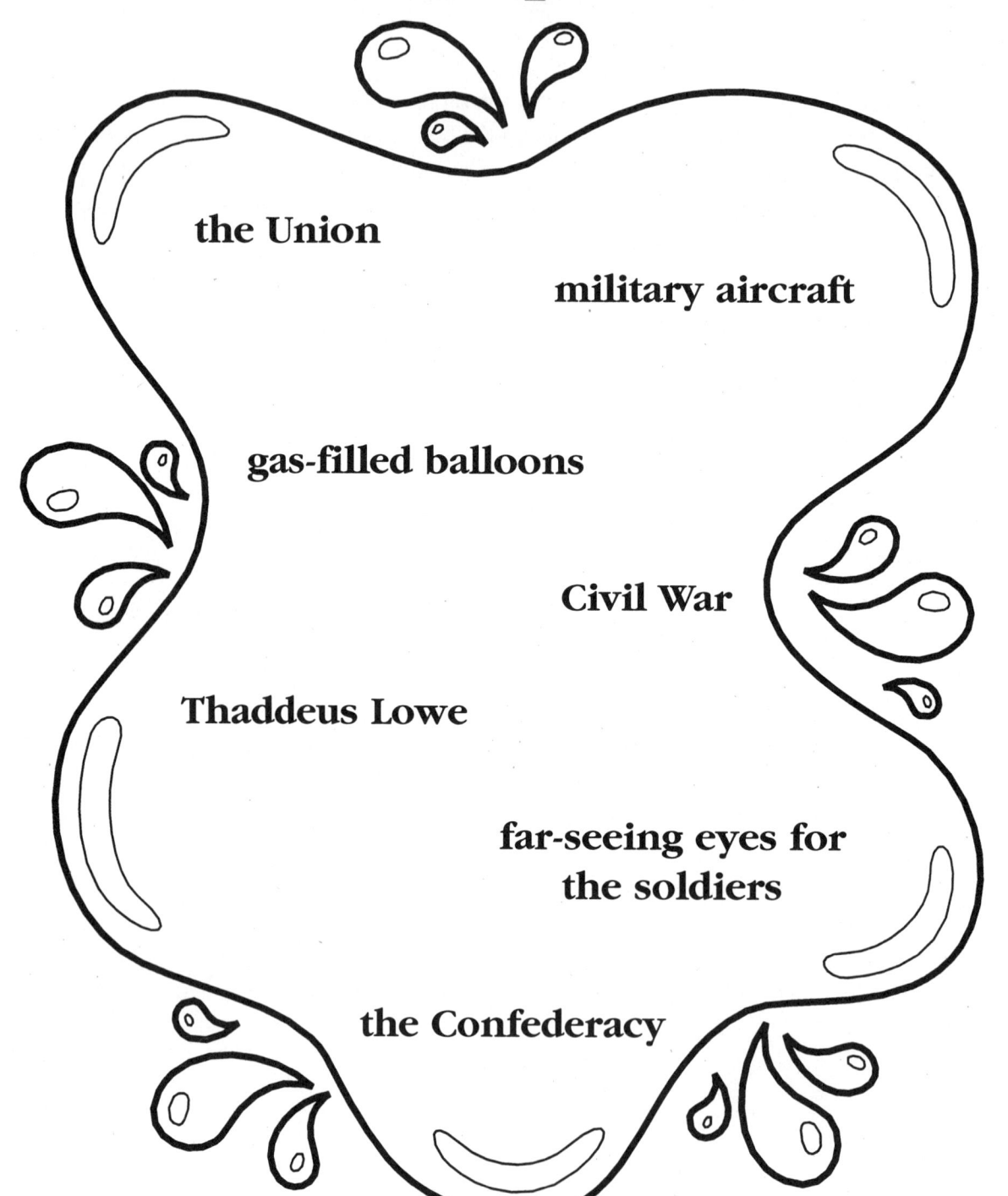

the Union

military aircraft

gas-filled balloons

Civil War

Thaddeus Lowe

far-seeing eyes for the soldiers

the Confederacy

BALLOONS in Battle

Military aircraft were used for the first time in United States history during the Civil War. However, airplanes weren't invented until 50 years after the war. What did the Civil War pilots fly? They flew huge gas-filled balloons. Pilots and their equipment rode in baskets attached to the bottom of each balloon.

Both the Union and the Confederacy tried using balloons in battle, but the Confederates had little success. They didn't have the materials or people needed to build and keep up an air force.

The Union Army did have a well-trained Balloon Corps. It was commanded by a professional balloonist named Thaddeus Lowe.

Like many Northerners, Lowe didn't take the war seriously at first. He was sure that the South's *rebellion* would end quickly and peacefully. The Confederates' revolt, Lowe believed, would not last. Lowe changed his mind, however, when he was taken prisoner by Confederate soldiers after a test flight to South Carolina.

Lowe was able to talk his way out of trouble, and he returned to the North. Then he set out to convince Union leaders that balloons would be of great value to their army.

To Lowe, the advantages, or good points, of using balloons were clear. Balloonists could see enemy soldiers and watch their movements. The balloonists could then signal their findings to soldiers on the ground. For the first time, officers would know everything that was happening on the battlefield.

Lowe's arguments were good, but it took a presidential order to get the Union Army to go along with the idea. Yet Lowe had set up seven balloon camps by early 1862. Where the *troops* went, the balloonists followed, acting as far-seeing eyes for the soldiers.

Lowe himself seemed to be everywhere, whenever he was needed. After an important battle at Fair Oaks, General A. W. Greely wrote: "It may be safely claimed that the Union Army was saved from destruction . . . by the frequent and accurate reports of Lowe."

One of Lowe's greatest compliments came from Confederate General E. P. Alexander, who wrote this about the Balloon Corps: "Even if the observers never saw anything, they [the Balloon Corps] would have been worth all they cost for the annoyance and delay they caused us in trying to keep our movements out of their sight."

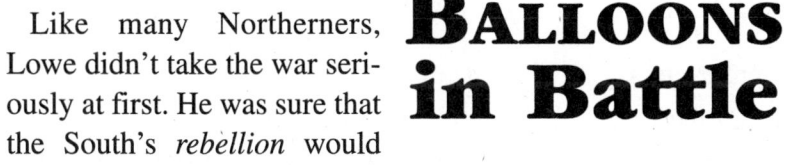

Name _____ Date _____

Balloons in Battle

Choose the best answer and mark the letter of your choice.

1. What is this article mostly about?
   A. types of balloons
   B. battles during the Civil War
   C. Thaddeus Lowe's capture during the Civil War
   D. balloons during the Civil War

2. Airplanes were invented
   F. after the Civil War.
   G. during the first year of the Civil War.
   H. before the Civil War.
   J. during the last year of the Civil War.

3. The Confederates had little success using balloons because
   A. they thought balloons were useless.
   B. they didn't know how to fly them.
   C. they didn't have the necessary materials or people.
   D. they didn't know how to make them.

4. In this article, the word *rebellion* means
   F. battles.
   G. revolt.
   H. agreement.
   J. secession.

5. Which of these is a fact presented in the article?
   A. The Civil War was not serious at first.
   B. Many Northerners did not take the war seriously at first.
   C. Many Southerners did not take the war seriously at first.
   D. From the start, Thaddeus Lowe thought the war was serious.

6. In this article, the word *troops* means
   F. balloonists.
   G. enemies.
   H. officials.
   J. soldiers.

7. The article gives you enough information to conclude that
   A. balloons were never used after the Civil War.
   B. balloons were useful to the Confederate Army.
   C. balloons were useful to the Union Army.
   D. balloons were not useful to either side.

8. The article gives you enough information to conclude that Thaddeus Lowe
   F. was with the Union Army at the Battle of Fair Oaks.
   G. never traveled with the troops.
   H. was a friend of Union General A. W. Greely.
   J. admired Confederate General E. P. Alexander.

UNIT 7
Abraham Lincoln, White House Father

A·B·C *Lesson Planner*

1. *Access*

- **READING STRATEGY:** Use the Anticipation Guide on page 54 before having small groups of students read the article. Write the statements on the board, or use the sheet as a copying master. Invite students to tell whether they agree or disagree with each statement. They can write their responses in their journals or learning logs. Do not expect students to know the answers. This activity is designed to help build interest, activate prior knowledge, and set purposes for reading.

2. *Build*

- Have students read the article, or read it aloud to them.
- As students read or after they finish reading the article, they may change their opinions about the statements. If they do, have them discuss why they revised their opinions, and have them state what they learned from their reading that allowed them to confirm or revise their opinions.

3. *Close*

- Have students complete the standardized-test-format questions after they read the article. (An item analysis that identifies the test objectives covered by each question, as well as an answer key, can be found on page 68.)
- **ART ACTIVITY:** Have students research some of the toys that were common during the Civil War period and make drawings of them.

Name _____ Date _____

Abraham Lincoln, White House Father

Anticipation Guide

Check One

	Agree	Disagree
1. Abraham Lincoln was sworn in as President on March 4, 1861.		
2. Lincoln was President during the Spanish-American War.		
3. Two of Lincoln's sons were named Tad and Willie.		
4. The President of the United States has the power to pardon soldiers.		
5. Lincoln hated the war.		

ABRAHAM LINCOLN
White House Father

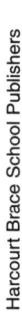

March 4, 1861, was an important day for Tad and Willie Lincoln. It was the day their father was sworn in as President of the United States. It was also the day they moved into the White House. Tad was 8 years old at the time, and Willie was 11.

Just a month after Abraham Lincoln became President, the United States was at war. A group of southern states had seceded from the Union, forming a new government called the Confederate States of America, or the *Confederacy*. Union troops were fighting the troops of those southern states. Lincoln was busy with military matters from morning until night. But he was never too busy for Tad and Willie.

One day, for example, Tad banged on his father's office door during an important meeting. Lincoln opened the door when he recognized Tad's special code of three short knocks and two long ones. Tad burst into the room, close to tears. He had just discovered that his pet turkey was about to be cooked for Christmas dinner. Lincoln came to the rescue. He told the cook to spare the turkey, even if it meant planning another dinner.

Tad and Willie spent many hours playing with toy soldiers. Sometimes, they got a little carried away. Once they pretended that a toy soldier had left his post. They sentenced the doll to death for *desertion,* but they couldn't bear to carry out the sentence. Finally, they asked their father for help.

As President, Lincoln had the power to pardon soldiers. He listened seriously as the boys presented the problem. Then, for the first time in United States history, a President wrote out a pardon for a doll: "The doll Jack is pardoned by order of the President. [Signed] A. Lincoln."

Abraham Lincoln hated the Civil War and the suffering it caused. He granted many requests for pardons. Once, during an advisory meeting with the President, the *secretary of war* complained that it was hard for the Army to control its soldiers with pardons being given. Lincoln thought about this for a while. Then he said, "Tad tells me I'm doing right, and Tad's advice is usually good."

Name _____ Date _____

Abraham Lincoln, White House Father

Choose the best answer and mark the letter of your choice.

1. What is this article mostly about?
   A. the kind of president Lincoln was
   B. the Civil War
   C. the kind of father Lincoln was
   D. life in the White House

2. March 4, 1861, was an important day for the nation because on that day
   F. Abraham Lincoln was sworn in as President.
   G. Tad and Willie Lincoln moved into the White House.
   H. the Confederacy was formed.
   J. the war ended.

3. In this article, the word *Confederacy* means
   A. a small group of southern soldiers.
   B. a new government formed by southern states.
   C. a group of border states.
   D. a newly formed southern army.

4. Which of these happened first?
   F. Union troops fought the Confederate troops.
   G. The Southern states seceded from the Union.
   H. Lincoln pardoned many soldiers.
   J. Lincoln was sworn in as President.

5. In this article, the word *desertion* means
   A. being assigned to desert patrol.
   B. spying for the enemy.
   C. leaving a military post without permission.
   D. sleeping while on duty.

6. The article gives you enough information to conclude that a *secretary of war* is someone who
   F. writes articles about wars.
   G. suggests how the President should handle military matters.
   H. pardons soldiers.
   J. has the power to declare war.

7. Which of these is a fact presented in the article?
   A. The secretary of war believed that the war was bad for the country.
   B. Lincoln granted many requests for pardons.
   C. Lincoln thought that the war was unnecessary.
   D. The secretary of war complained about Lincoln's taking advice from other people.

8. The article gives you enough information to conclude that
   F. Lincoln was a great President.
   G. Lincoln was a loving father.
   H. Lincoln had little time for his family.
   J. Tad and Willie had many friends.

UNIT 8
Bell's Telephone

A·B·C LESSON PLANNER

1. Access

- **READING STRATEGY:** Use the Word Splash on page 58 to help students make predictions about the article. Write the words on the board, or use the sheet as a copying master. Invite students to predict how each word or phrase relates to the invention of the telephone. Students can write their predictions in their journals or learning logs. Do not expect students to know the answers. This activity is designed to help build interest, activate prior knowledge, and set purposes for reading.

2. Build

- Have students read the article, or read it aloud to them.
- As students read or after they finish reading the article, they may change their Word Splash predictions. Have them identify the predictions that were correct, and have them state what they have learned from reading the article.

3. Close

- Have students complete the standardized-test-format questions after they read the article. (An item analysis that identifies the test objectives covered by each question, as well as an answer key, can be found on page 68.)
- **MATHEMATICS ACTIVITY:** Have students find the current prices of long-distance telephone calls. Invite students to use the information they find to create mathematical problems about long-distance calls.

Name _____ Date _____

Bell's Telephone
Word Splash

experimenting with homemade telephone

Thomas Watson

Bell Telephone Company

telephone lines

a new age in communication

coast-to-coast telephone conversation

invention

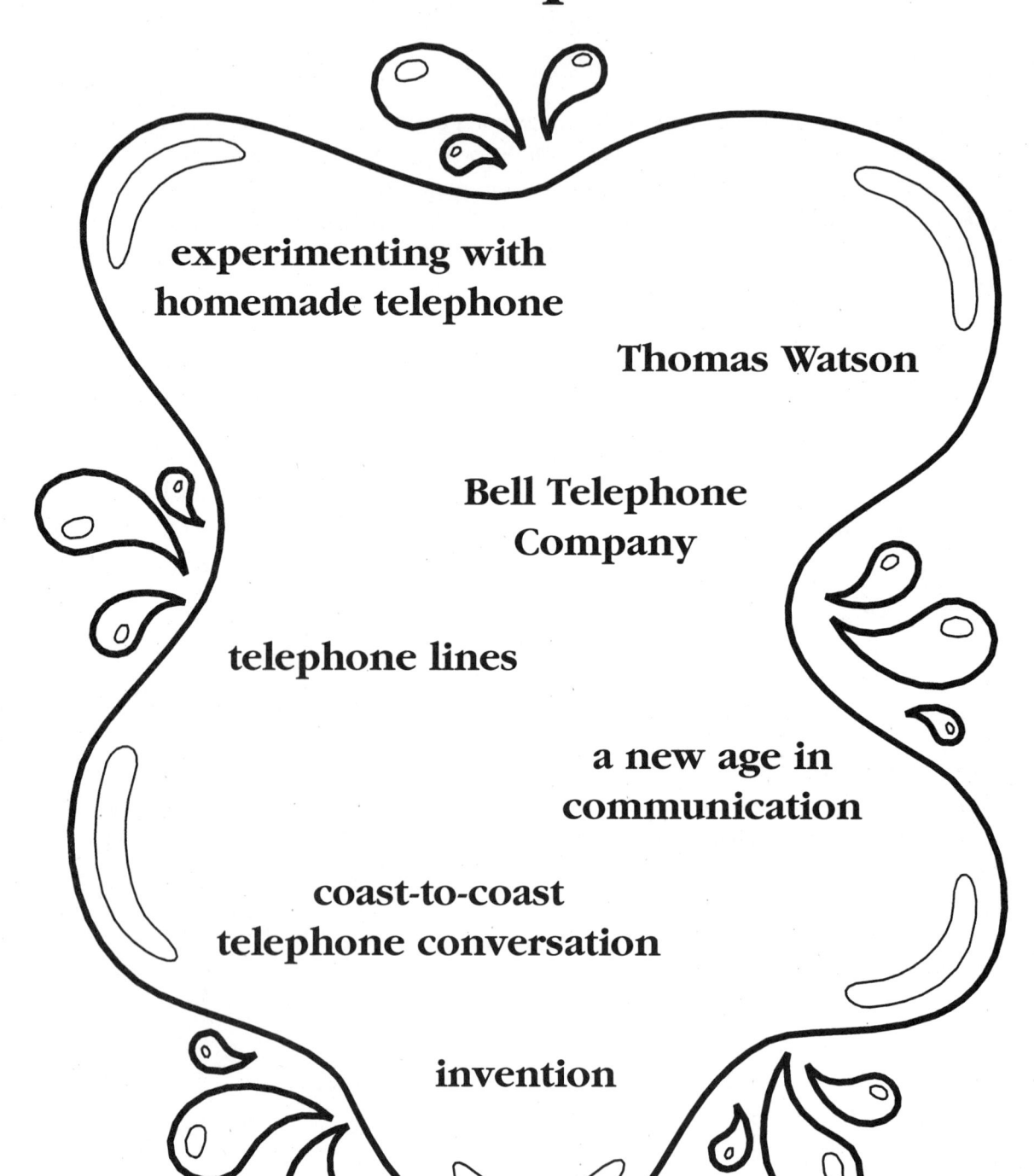

BELL'S TELEPHONE

The first message delivered over the telephone came about as the result of an accident. The speaker was Alexander Graham Bell. The listener was his assistant, Thomas Watson. The men were in separate rooms, experimenting with Bell's homemade telephone. They already knew how to send sounds across telephone wires. Now they were trying to send words.

Suddenly, Bell spilled some acid on himself, burning his clothes. Without thinking, he cried out: "Mr. Watson, come here. I want you!" Watson came rushing in. He had heard Bell's voice over the telephone! The date was March 10, 1876. It was the first day of a new age in communication.

For Bell, there was just one problem. He didn't have the money to start a telephone company of his own. He tried to sell his invention to the Western Union Telegraph Company, but company leaders weren't interested. They thought the telephone was just a clever toy.

Bell was not easily discouraged. He found people to invest in his invention. One of them was Gardiner Hubbard, Bell's future father-in-law.

The Bell Telephone Company was finally formed on July 9, 1877. Two days later Bell married Mabel Hubbard. As a wedding present, he gave her most of his *stock* in the new company, keeping only ten shares for himself.

Business was good right from the start, even though the first telephones were hard to use. They carried sound for only a few miles, and people had to shout to be heard. Over time, however, the problems were solved and improvements were made. People finally had a way to communicate without leaving their homes or writing letters.

By 1915 telephone lines stretched across the nation. On January 25 of that year, Alexander Graham Bell and Thomas Watson had the first coast-to-coast telephone conversation.

Bell, who was in New York, made the call to Watson, who was in San Francisco. "Mr. Watson, come here. I want you!" said Bell, repeating the very first telephone message he had said to his old friend and assistant.

The call took 23 minutes to get through to San Francisco, and it cost $20.70. Today, it would take less than 23 seconds to connect and would cost less than $2.00.

Name _____ Date _____

Bell's Telephone

Choose the best answer and mark the letter of your choice.

1. What is this article mostly about?
   A. the Bell Telephone Company
   B. Alexander Graham Bell and the telephone
   C. Alexander Graham Bell and Thomas Watson
   D. telephone company stock

2. March 10, 1876, was the day that
   F. Bell and Watson first experimented with the telephone.
   G. the Bell Telephone Company was formed.
   H. the first coast-to-coast telephone call took place.
   J. Bell and Watson first communicated by telephone.

3. Which of these is a fact presented in the article?
   A. Leaders of the Western Union Telegraph Company thought the telephone was just a toy.
   B. The first telephone was a clever toy.
   C. People treated telephones like toys.
   D. Bell's investors thought the telephone was a toy.

4. Because Bell found people to invest in his invention,
   F. the Bell Telephone Company was formed.
   G. he sold stocks to his friends.
   H. he got married.
   J. he gave the company to his wife.

5. In this article, the word *stock* means
   A. a supply of goods.
   B. an investment.
   C. a wedding present.
   D. a share in a company or business.

6. What is the main idea of the sixth paragraph?
   F. The telephone was used to call people who lived a few miles away.
   G. Early telephones had problems.
   H. The telephone business was good because people wanted other ways to communicate.
   J. Using the telephone required people to shout.

7. The first coast-to-coast phone call was made
   A. in 1876.
   B. in 1915.
   C. before 1900.
   D. sometime between 1900 and 1914.

8. The article gives you enough information to conclude that telephone calls today are
   F. harder and more expensive to make than they were in the past.
   G. slower and more expensive to make than they were in the past.
   H. faster and less expensive to make than they were in the past.
   J. slower and less expensive to make than they were in the past.

UNIT 8
Edison's Talking Machine

A·B·C Lesson Planner

1. Access

- **READING STRATEGY:** Use the Anticipation Guide on page 62 before having small groups of students read the article. Write the statements on the board, or use the sheet as a copying master. Invite students to tell whether they agree or disagree with each statement. They can write their responses in their journals or learning logs. Do not expect students to know the answers. This activity is designed to help build interest, activate prior knowledge, and set purposes for reading.

2. Build

- Have students read the article, or read it aloud to them.
- As students read or after they finish reading the article, they may change their opinions about the statements. If they do, have them discuss why they revised their opinions, and have them state what they learned from their reading that allowed them to confirm or revise their opinions.

3. Close

- Have students complete the standardized-test-format questions after they read the article. (An item analysis that identifies the test objectives covered by each question, as well as an answer key, can be found on page 68.)
- **SCIENCE ACTIVITY:** Have students research other inventions made by Thomas Edison. Invite students to find five facts about each invention. Students can then create an invention guessing game based on the facts.

Name _____ Date _____

Edison's Talking Machine
Anticipation Guide

Check One

	Agree	Disagree
1. Thomas Edison's favorite invention was the light bulb.		
2. The first phonograph recording was a verse from a nursery rhyme.		
3. The phonograph made Edison famous throughout the world.		
4. Edison was trying to improve the telegraph when he got the idea for the phonograph.		
5. Edison thought of many different uses for the phonograph.		

Edison's Talking Machine

In a period of 60 years, Thomas Alva Edison worked on more than 1,000 inventions. Which was his favorite? The phonograph was the one. "This is my baby," he once told a reporter, "and I expect it to grow up and . . . support me in my old age."

Edison didn't set out to invent the phonograph. He was trying to improve the telephone when he came up with an idea for a machine that could record voices. He worked on the machine for a year. Then, on December 6, 1877, he was ready to test it. He recited this familiar nursery rhyme for the test:

Mary had a little lamb,
Its fleece was white as snow,
And everywhere that Mary went
The lamb was sure to go.

When he finished speaking, Edison played the recording. It repeated his every word. Edison was amazed. He had hoped the machine would work, but he had not expected it to work so well! "I was never so taken aback in all my life," he said later. "I was always afraid of things that worked the first time."

People came from all over to try the phonograph, or "talking machine," as it was called in its early days. It made Edison famous throughout the world, and he became known as the Wizard of Menlo Park.

Menlo Park, New Jersey, was where Thomas Edison had his research *laboratory.* Today many large corporations have research laboratories. Edison's lab was the first of its kind in the United States. It was so impressive that many people who saw it decided to *invest* in Edison's inventions. Buying shares of his businesses seemed like a sure way to make a profit.

It was at Menlo Park that Edison developed the electric light bulb. That project, and several others, took about ten years of his time. But by 1886, he was back at work on his favorite invention, the phonograph.

Thomas Edison made many improvements to the phonograph. He came up with many new ways to use it. He thought the phonograph could be used in advertisements, toys, and even talking books for the blind. He also predicted other ways it could be used. Edison was not really a wizard, but when it came to the phonograph, every prediction he made came true.

Name_____ Date_____

Edison's Talking Machine

Choose the best answer and mark the letter of your choice.

1. What is this article mostly about?
   A. Thomas Alva Edison and the electric light bulb
   B. phonographs today
   C. Edison's research laboratory
   D. Thomas Alva Edison and the phonograph

2. When Edison said that he expected the phonograph to support him in his old age, he meant that he expected
   F. to earn a lot of money from the phonograph.
   G. the phonograph to be his last invention.
   H. the phonograph to be his only invention.
   J. to sell the phonograph to a corporation.

3. In this article, the word *laboratory* means
   A. a secret room in an office.
   B. a laundry area in a home.
   C. a place where research goes on.
   D. a room where meetings are held.

4. The first phonographs were called
   F. Edison's machines.
   G. recording machines.
   H. voice machines.
   J. talking machines.

5. Edison became known as the Wizard of Menlo Park because he
   A. tried to improve the telephone.
   B. invented the phonograph.
   C. built the first research laboratory.
   D. got people to invest in his inventions.

6. In this article, the word *invest* means
   F. make a profit from a famous invention.
   G. sell an invention to a large group of people who will resell it.
   H. buy shares of a business in the hope of making a profit.
   J. buy a company that makes something that people want in the hope of making a profit.

7. Thomas Edison is also known for his invention of
   A. the telephone.
   B. the electric light bulb.
   C. the telegraph.
   D. electricity.

8. What is the main idea of the last paragraph?
   F. The phonograph has many uses.
   G. The phonograph needs to be improved.
   H. Edison could predict the future.
   J. It took ten years to develop the phonograph.

ITEM ANALYSES AND ANSWER KEYS

Unit 1

BURIED TREASURE

Item Analysis: 1. Identify the best summary; 2. Recall supporting facts and details; 3. Identify cause and effect; 4. Identify cause and effect; 5. Make inferences and generalizations; 6. Use context clues; 7. Make inferences and generalizations; 8. Predict probable future outcomes.

Answers: 1. B; 2. J; 3. A; 4. G; 5. C; 6. H; 7. B; 8. J

CORN—THE BREAD OF LIFE

Item Analysis: 1. Identify the best summary; 2. Identify specialized/technical terms; 3. Identify cause and effect; 4. Recall supporting facts and details; 5. Draw conclusions; 6. Identify compound words; 7. Identify the main idea; 8. Use context clues.

Answers: 1. B; 2. J; 3. A; 4. H; 5. C; 6. J; 7. B; 8. F

Unit 2

A DANGEROUS CROSSING

Item Analysis: 1. Identify the best summary; 2. Use context clues; 3. Identify cause and effect; 4. Distinguish between fact and nonfact; 5. Identify compound words; 6. Identify specialized/technical terms; 7. Recall supporting facts and details; 8. Draw conclusions.

Answers: 1. C; 2. J; 3. D; 4. G; 5. A; 6. G; 7. D; 8. H

THE STORY OF CHOCOLATE

Item Analysis: 1. Identify the best summary; 2. Recall supporting facts and details; 3. Identify sequence; 4. Identify cause and effect; 5. Use context clues; 6. Recall supporting facts and details; 7. Distinguish between fact and nonfact; 8. Predict probable future outcomes.

Answers: 1. A; 2. G; 3. B; 4. J; 5. C; 6. H; 7. D; 8. G

Unit 3

BARN RAISING
Item Analysis: 1. Identify the main idea; 2. Use context clues; 3. Identify specialized/technical terms; 4. Identify sequence; 5. Recall supporting facts and details; 6. Recall supporting facts and details; 7. Identify cause and effect; 8. Draw conclusions.

Answers: 1. B; 2. J; 3. B; 4. F; 5. A; 6. H; 7. B; 8. J

SCHOOL DAYS
Item Analysis: 1. Identify the best summary; 2. Identify cause and effect; 3. Identify specialized/technical terms; 4. Identify compound words; 5. Recall supporting facts and details; 6. Identify sequence; 7. Use context clues; 8. Make inferences and generalizations.

Answers: 1. C; 2. F; 3. B; 4. J; 5. B; 6. H; 7. D; 8. F

Unit 4

BENJAMIN FRANKLIN: WRITER, SCIENTIST, STATESMAN
Item Analysis: 1. Identify the best summary; 2. Draw conclusions; 3. Recall supporting facts and details; 4. Identify compound words; 5. Identify cause and effect; 6. Predict probable future outcomes; 7. Use context clues; 8. Use context clues.

Answers: 1. C; 2. H; 3. B; 4. F; 5. A; 6. J; 7. B; 8. G

THE SPIRIT OF 1776
Item Analysis: 1. Identify the best summary; 2. Use context clues; 3. Identify the main idea; 4. Identify cause and effect; 5. Identify compound words; 6. Identify sequence; 7. Recall supporting facts and details; 8. Make inferences and generalizations.

Answers: 1. B; 2. F; 3. C; 4. J; 5. A; 6. H; 7. B; 8. J

Unit 5

FATHER OF THE CONSTITUTION
Item Analysis: 1. Identify the best summary; 2. Identify cause and effect; 3. Identify sequence; 4. Recall supporting facts and details; 5. Recall supporting facts and details; 6. Use context clues; 7. Use context clues; 8. Draw conclusions.

Answers: 1. D; 2. F; 3. C; 4. G; 5. D; 6. G; 7. D; 8. F

ABIGAIL ADAMS, A WOMAN AHEAD OF HER TIME
Item Analysis: 1. Identify the best summary; 2. Identify compound words; 3. Identify specialized/technical terms; 4. Identify cause and effect; 5. Recall supporting facts and details; 6. Identify sequence; 7. Distinguish between fact and nonfact; 8. Draw conclusions.

Answers: 1. B; 2. F; 3. A; 4. H; 5. B; 6. J; 7. B; 8. J

Unit 6

GOLD FEVER
Item Analysis: 1. Identify the best summary; 2. Draw conclusions; 3. Use context clues; 4. Recall supporting facts and details; 5. Identify cause and effect; 6. Identify specialized/technical terms; 7. Distinguish between fact and nonfact; 8. Draw conclusions.

Answers: 1. D; 2. F; 3. C; 4. G; 5. B; 6. F; 7. C; 8. G

AN AMERICAN STORY
Item Analysis: 1. Identify the best summary; 2. Use context clues; 3. Recall supporting facts and details; 4. Identify sequence; 5. Identify cause and effect; 6. Draw conclusions; 7. Distinguish between fact and nonfact; 8. Predict probable future outcomes.

Answers: 1. C; 2. J; 3. D; 4. G; 5. A; 6. G; 7. C; 8. F

Unit 7

BALLOONS IN BATTLE
Item Analysis: 1. Identify the best summary; 2. Identify sequence; 3. Identify cause and effect; 4. Use context clues; 5. Distinguish between fact and nonfact; 6. Identify specialized/technical terms; 7. Draw conclusions; 8. Draw conclusions.

Answers: 1. D; 2. F; 3. C; 4. G; 5. B; 6. J; 7. C; 8. F

ABRAHAM LINCOLN, WHITE HOUSE FATHER
Item Analysis: 1. Identify the best summary; 2. Identify cause and effect; 3. Use context clues; 4. Identify sequence; 5. Use context clues; 6. Identify specialized/technical terms; 7. Distinguish between fact and nonfact; 8. Draw conclusions.

Answers: 1. C; 2. F; 3. B; 4. J; 5. C; 6. G; 7. B; 8. G

Unit 8

BELL'S TELEPHONE
Item Analysis: 1. Identify the best summary; 2. Recall supporting facts and details; 3. Distinguish between fact and nonfact; 4. Identify cause and effect; 5. Use context clues; 6. Identify the main idea; 7. Identify sequence; 8. Draw conclusions.

Answers: 1. B; 2. J; 3. A; 4. F; 5. D; 6. H; 7. B; 8. H

EDISON'S TALKING MACHINE
Item Analysis: 1. Identify the best summary; 2. Draw conclusions; 3. Identify specialized/technical terms; 4. Recall supporting facts and details; 5. Identify cause and effect; 6. Use context clues; 7. Recall supporting facts and details; 8. Identify the main idea.

Answers: 1. D; 2. F; 3. C; 4. J; 5. B; 6. H; 7. B; 8. F

READING COMPREHENSION STRATEGIES

Word Webs

Before reading an article, create a word web to introduce a vocabulary word or concept. Write the concept or vocabulary word in the center circle of the web, and invite students to brainstorm related words or concepts for the other circles. Word webs can be created as a whole-class activity or as small-group activities.

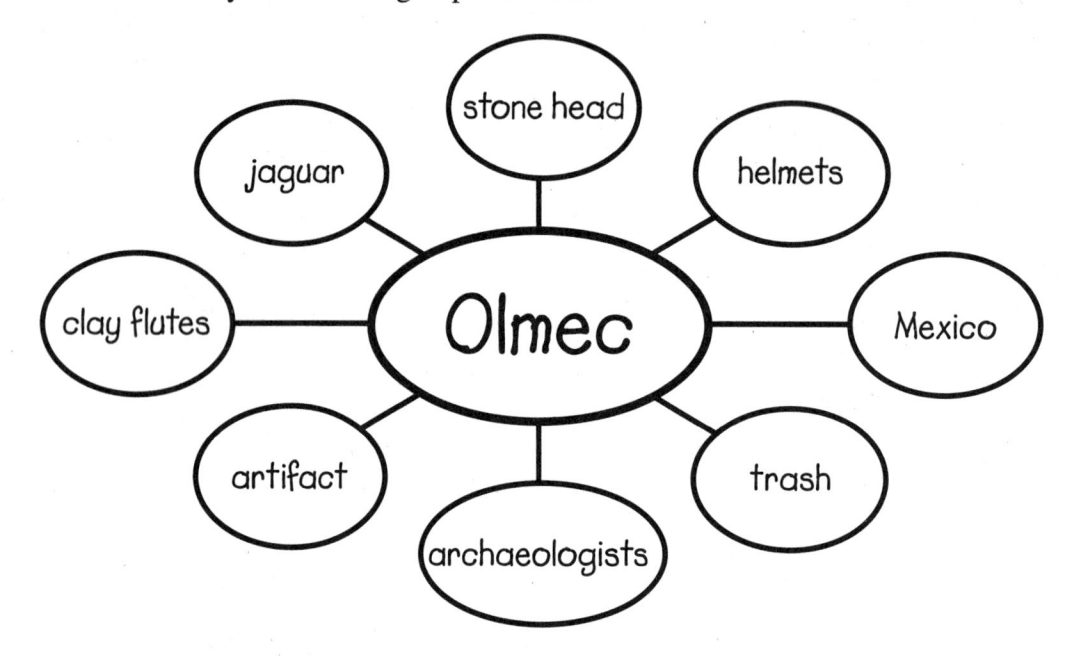

A word web with "Olmec" in the center, connected to: stone head, helmets, Mexico, trash, archaeologists, artifact, clay flutes, jaguar.

K-W-L Charts

Before reading an article, invite students to create a K-W-L chart like the one below. Students can fill in columns one and two before reading and column three after reading.

What I Know	What I Want to Know	What I Learned
The Mayflower set sail for America in 1620.	What was the crossing like for the Pilgrims?	Passengers were crowded into a very small, dark space where they ate, slept, and prayed; there was no fresh air.

Anticipation Guides

Before reading an article, prepare a set of five or six statements that students can classify as **agree** or **disagree**. You may wish to write these statements on the board or on an overhead transparency. Then have the whole class come to consensus about whether they agree or disagree with the statements. After reading, students can discuss how accurate their classifications were.

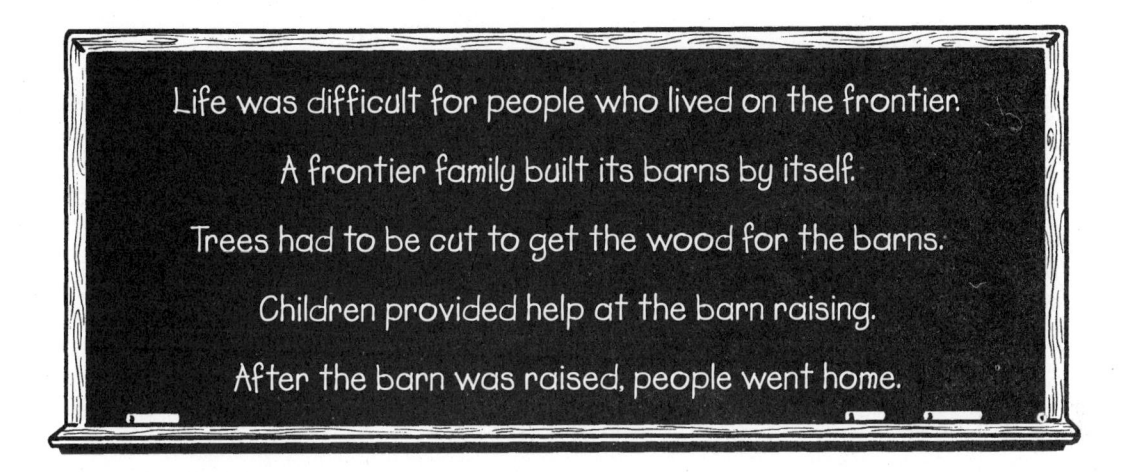

> Life was difficult for people who lived on the frontier.
>
> A frontier family built its barns by itself.
>
> Trees had to be cut to get the wood for the barns.
>
> Children provided help at the barn raising.
>
> After the barn was raised, people went home.

Other kinds of anticipation guides can be developed to focus on vocabulary words or to present statements that students have to make predictions about.

Preview/Prediction Charts

To help students preview an article and make predictions about the content they will read, create a chart like the one below. Model this chart on an overhead transparency or on the board, and invite students to make one like it in their journals or learning logs. Students can record their predictions before reading and verify or revise them as they read.

Prediction	Clues	What Really Happened
Ben Franklin's Plan of Union set the stage for the unification of the colonies.	Colonists liked the idea but were not ready.	Colonists continued to ask Franklin for advice; they were ready for his proposal for a treaty after the Revolution.

Reading Support and Test Preparation **71**

Photos and Illustrations

Remind students that photos and illustrations can help them understand the text on the page. Very often photos and illustrations are used to clarify concepts or vocabulary words that are discussed in the text. Frequently, point out illustrations and photos to students and ask them to discuss what they see. Use maps provided in the book as well as maps in the classroom to help students gain geographical understanding.

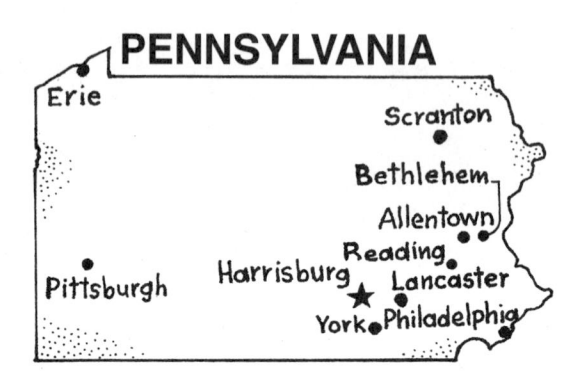

PENNSYLVANIA

Erie
Scranton
Bethlehem
Allentown
Reading
Pittsburgh   Harrisburg   Lancaster
York Philadelphia

Venn Diagrams

Before, during, and after reading, students can compare and contrast information by using Venn diagrams. The circle on the left can be used for information unique to one topic, the circle on the right for information unique to another related topic, and the overlapping part for common information.

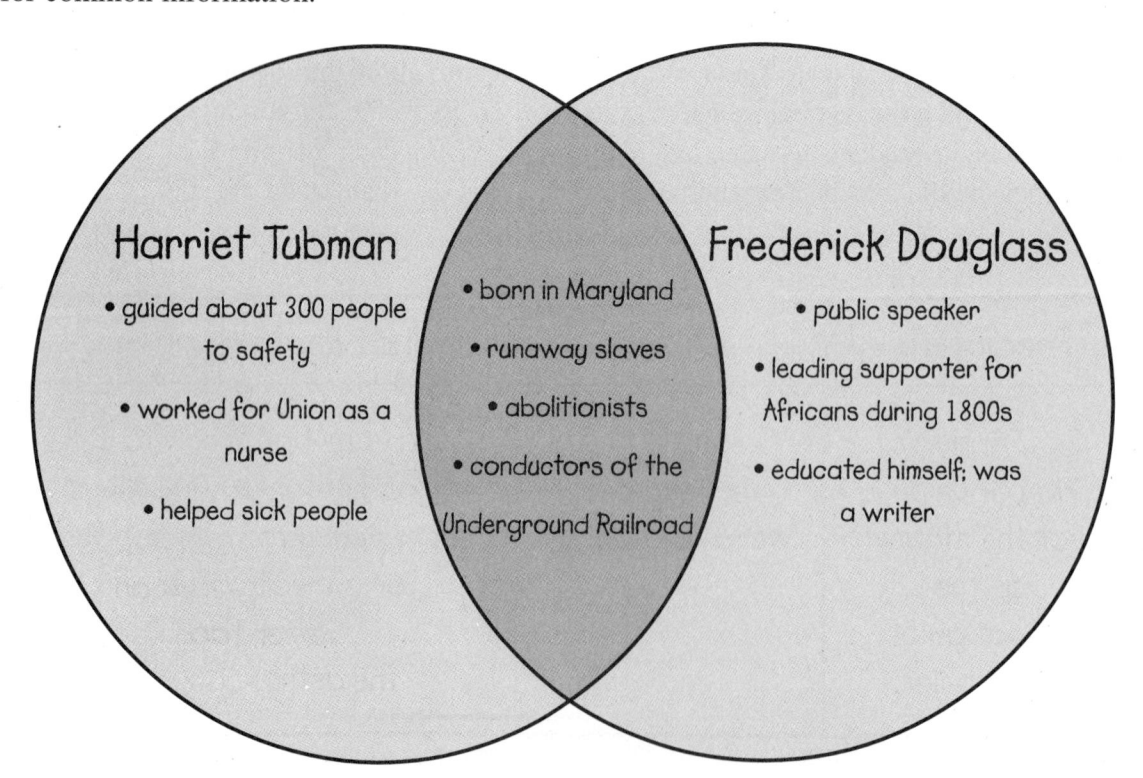

Harriet Tubman
- guided about 300 people to safety
- worked for Union as a nurse
- helped sick people

- born in Maryland
- runaway slaves
- abolitionists
- conductors of the Underground Railroad

Frederick Douglass
- public speaker
- leading supporter for Africans during 1800s
- educated himself; was a writer

72 *Reading Support and Test Preparation*

Flow Charts—Visual Representations

Before, during, and after reading, students can benefit from using visual frameworks, such as flow charts, to organize the text. Visual frameworks can be set up to classify information, compare or contrast information, or organize information into sequence. The content of the lesson will dictate what kind of visual framework you develop. The flow chart below works well for classifying historical information.

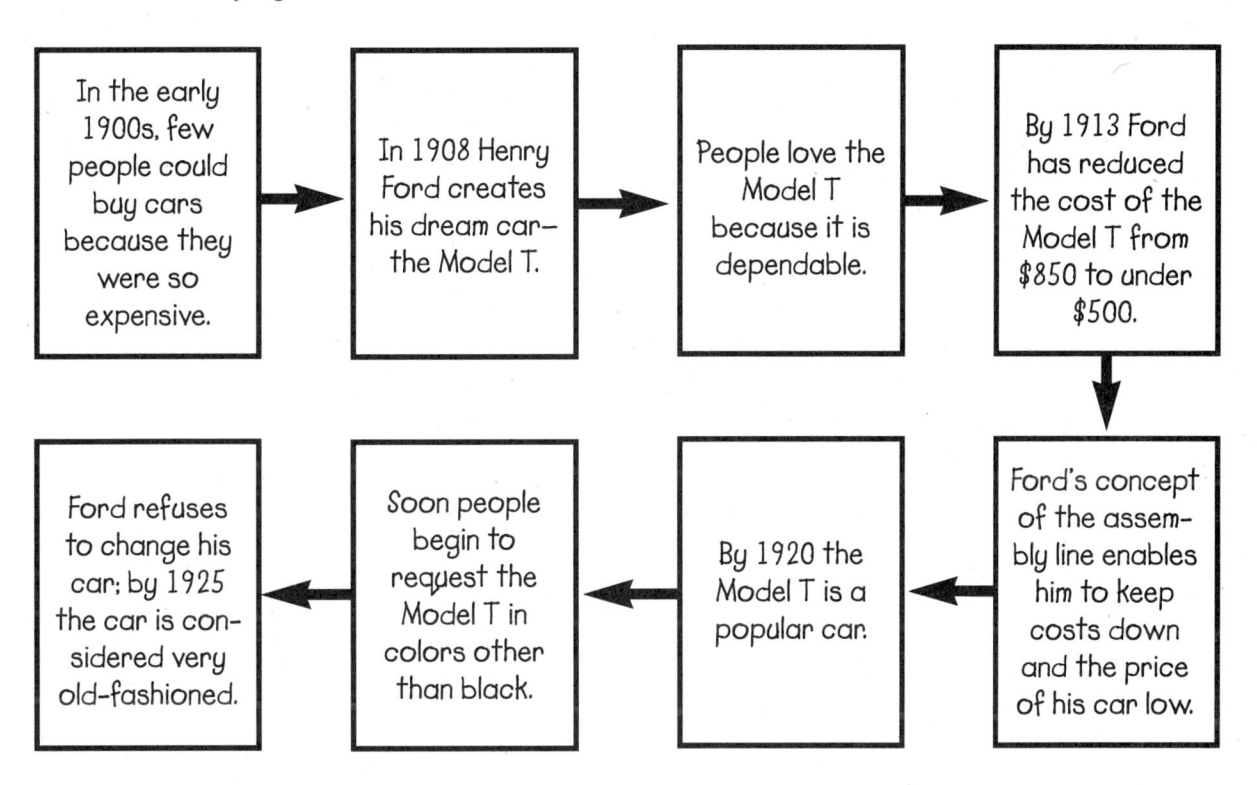

In the early 1900s, few people could buy cars because they were so expensive. → In 1908 Henry Ford creates his dream car—the Model T. → People love the Model T because it is dependable. → By 1913 Ford has reduced the cost of the Model T from $850 to under $500. ↓

Ford refuses to change his car; by 1925 the car is considered very old-fashioned. ← Soon people begin to request the Model T in colors other than black. ← By 1920 the Model T is a popular car. ← Ford's concept of the assembly line enables him to keep costs down and the price of his car low.

Cause/Effect Charts

Assist students in seeing cause-and-effect relationships by having them create cause/effect charts. After reading an article or a lesson, students can create a chart like the one below.

Cause	Effect
Early space food is packed in aluminum tubes that have to be squeezed like toothpaste tubes.	Astronauts complain about the food on their missions.
Space missions become longer.	NASA begins to work on getting better food for the astronauts.

Reading Support and Test Preparation

Hands-On Activity

Hands-on activities are an ideal way to reinforce social studies content. Here's an activity that will help students review the most important events in a unit of study through a tactile experience.

UNITED STATES HISTORY: THE GAME

Materials (one set for each student):
- 1 8 1/2" x 11" sheet of white poster board or white paper
- several different color fine-tip markers
- 4 small items to use as game pieces, such as a nickel, a penny, an eraser, and a paper clip

1. Tell the class that it is time to review their present unit of study. One way to do this is to make a game of it. And that is exactly what they will do for this unit.

2. Distribute the materials. Tell students that they should make a board game that includes the content of the unit. Students should begin planning their game by first listing the important events of the unit.

3. Next, have students make a series of spaces or blocks on their sheet of poster board or paper. Their spaces or blocks should take the form of a route. They should label the first space **Start** and the last one **End.**

4. In each space students should write about an event in the unit and include a game instruction. For example, one space might read: "The Declaration of Independence was signed in 1776. Go forward two spaces."

5. Have students check their games to be sure that the game can be played successfully. Ask students to correct any problems.

6. Once the games are complete, have groups of students play each game. Students can use their small objects as game pieces. Sit back and watch as students review the unit and have fun at the same time.

Name _____ Date _____

Word Web

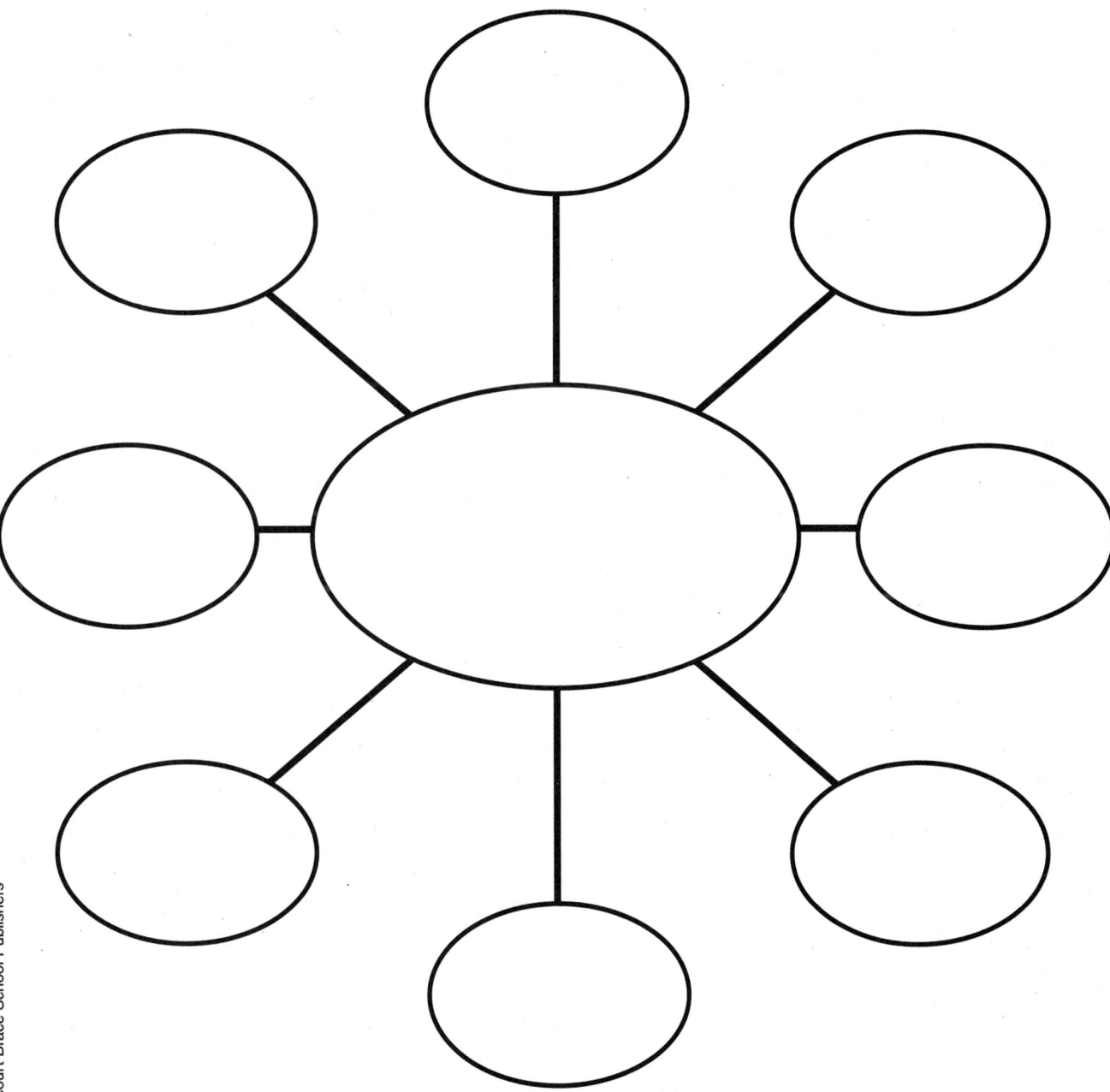

Name _____ Date _____

K-W-L Chart

What I Know	What I Want to Know	What I Learned

Name _____ Date _____

Prediction Chart

Prediction	Clues	What Really Happened

Name _____ Date _____

Flow Chart

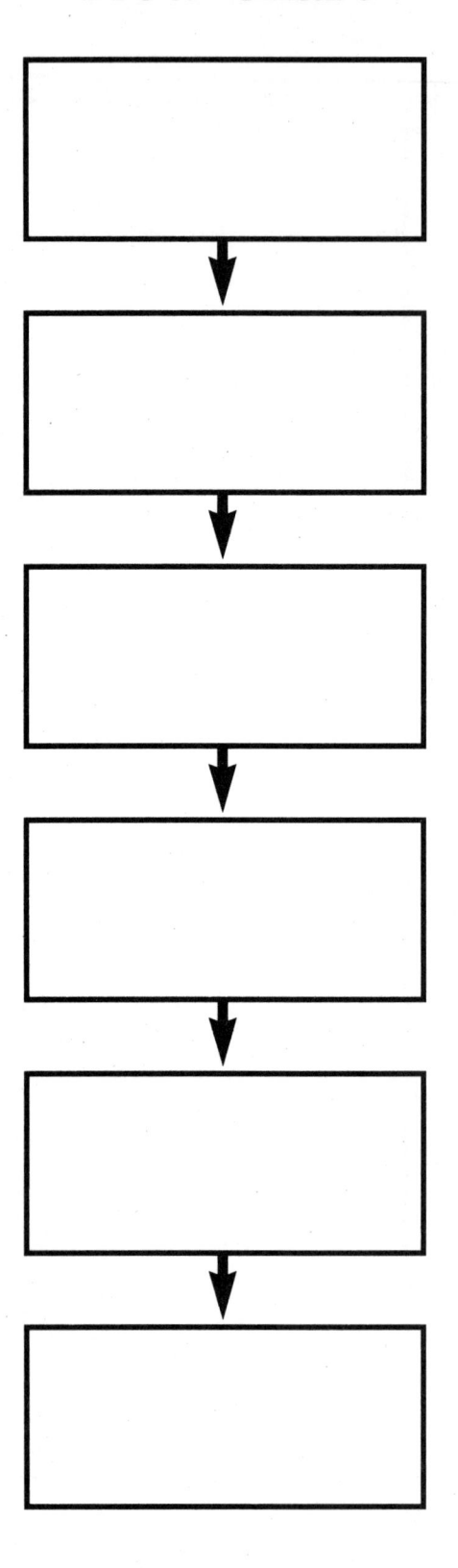

Name _____ Date _____

Venn Diagram

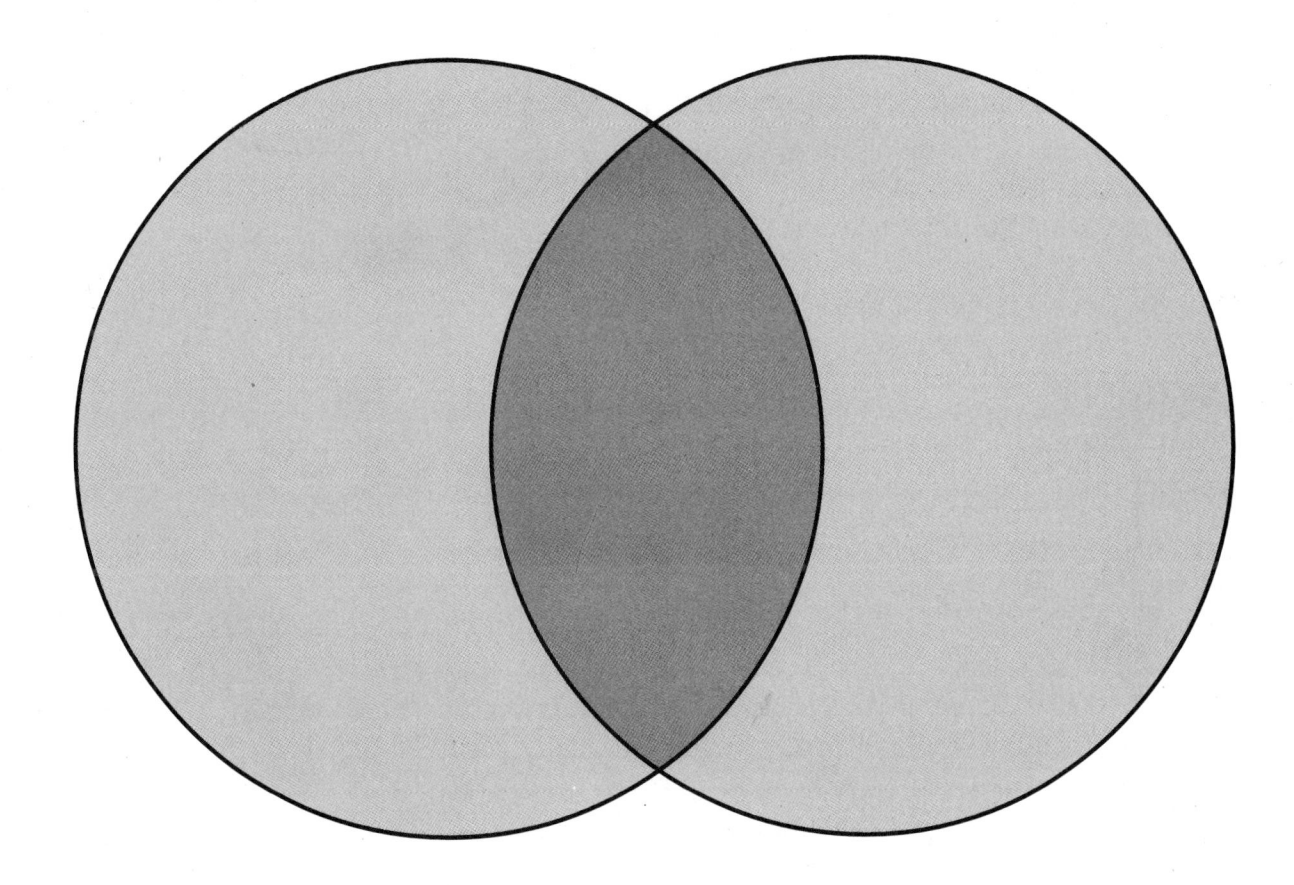